Personal Consecration
or Conditions of Discipleship
A Series of Bible Studies

by
Rev. Hubert Brooke, M.A.

**Personal Consecration
or Conditions of Discipleship**
A series of Bible studies
by Rev. Hubert Brooke, M.A.,

First printing, 1897

Scripture quotations are from the King James Version.
All references to Greek or Hebrew manuscripts have been omitted.
A minimal amount of archaic words have been updated for the modern
day reader and a few words with British spellings have been changed to
American English.

Copyright 2015 by Victory Baptist Press

ISBN 978-1-940791-05-0

Current edition published in 2015 by
Victory Baptist Press
Milton, Florida — USA

Cover design and layout by Trinity Lorimer

Contents

Chapter 1
The Subject Defined

"It is good to be zealously affected always in *a* good *thing."*
(Galatians 4:18)

IT is a healthy sign, and a promise of good times for the church of Christ, that so many of its members are keenly interested in the subject of holiness and its kindred doctrines. For many years past, great stress has been laid upon the elementary lessons of the gospel, the topics of "repentance toward God and faith toward our Lord Jesus Christ," in much of the evangelistic and mission preaching of the day; and such stress was very necessary, since those elements had been widely obscured or ignored. But to a great extent, the logical consequences of those elementary lessons have not been made equally prominent. Conversion and the coming of the soul to the Saviour have been so exclusively insisted upon, that consecration and the soul's following of the Saviour have been left out of sight. The result has been a partially developed Christian life and experience in individuals and churches. The infantile stage, the babe in Christ, has been regarded as the normal condition of Christian existence and knowledge; pardon and reconciliation to God were taken as the sum and climax of the gospel; personal salvation seemed to be reckoned as the alpha and omega of religion. Such a practical disregard of the principles and conditions of Christian growth and progress resulted in defective experience, curtailed development, feeble service, little power. Happily, that state of things is beginning to pass away. The widespread and much blessed work of missions to the unconverted is being rightly and wisely supplemented by conferences of Christian workers, conventions for the promotion of holiness, special services for the deepening of spiritual life, missionary missions and kindred efforts. These all serve to express the needful confession, that conversion and conscious peace with God are the starting point for the Christian life and service, not the goal at the end, nor the limit of attainment therein.

Personal Consecration

No doubt such interest as is now being aroused naturally brings with it some of the storms of controversy which have also raged around the topics of conversion and the true elements and beginnings of that life. This need neither disturb nor surprise the earnest Christian. It is rather to be considered a cheering sign, that there is a truth and a testimony worth contending for. When the controversy has run its course, it will surely end in a firmer conviction about the essentials under discussion, an avoidance of possible excrescences and a deeper knowledge of the real truth. It is only when we have to defend our possessions that we come to define their real value and to decide what can be discarded and what must be held fast at all costs. That perfect agreement cannot be attained about the question of personal consecration and holiness, among those who are equally true in their faith in Christ, should neither discourage us from the search after holiness, nor hinder the soul's energy in its pursuit. God has commanded it: "Be ye holy; for I am holy." Let that suffice for every obedient Christian. What He commands, we must seek to attain. Better the honest attempt with partial success, than the indolent excuse that failure is certain and the attempt useless. As soon as the topic of holiness is deliberately chosen as a matter of vital concern to the Christian; as soon as we seek a clear understanding of its meaning and possibility in actual experience, there meets us a long list of important questions raised.

The very mention of which indicates how widely divergent are the tenets of various schools of thought upon this subject. And if we leave aside even the wider and larger subject of holiness in its fullness, we find a sufficiency of disturbing questions about the one branch of it, which we are specially now concerned with: that of personal consecration. Is it a single act, or a continual process? Is it absolute and finished by one decisive step of the soul, or is it a progressive development, lifelong and ever incomplete? Is it a reality existing as a matter of course in all Christians alike; or does it by its presence or absence create a distinction between different people who are equally entitled to that name? Is it included in the experience of conversion, or is it a separate or separable stage of soul growth? When once existing in the soul, is it necessarily permanent, or may it be intermittent in its reality and power?

These questions are not mere theological phrases, of solely academic interest and of small concern to the ordinary servant of God. They are of deepest importance to each honest soul that desires to serve God thoroughly. Mistaken or uncertain doctrine will here, as in every other branch of divine truth, result in mistaken or uncertain practice. "For as he thinketh in his heart, so is he." But in seeking for an answer to such questions, it is well to remember that truth, like the city of Zion, has more sides than one; and he who would know the truth or the city must "go round about her: tell the towers thereof." In our search for a solution to the series of alternatives suggested above, we may find ourselves constrained to assent to both, to deny that they are necessarily opposing ideas, and to conclude that they represent often the initial act and the continuous experience of the same doctrine and theory. It is, therefore, of great importance to start with a clear definition of the subject under discussion. If two disputants are using the same terms in different senses, it is obvious that they can never attain to agreement in their conclusions.

A simple illustration of the need for definition may be found in the vexed question of sinless perfection. Wesley's teaching on holiness is supposed to represent a state of sinlessness as practically attainable here on earth. Whether that is a logical deduction from his writings or not, it certainly seems to be plainly taught by some who follow his theories in the present day. But let there be first the all-important agreement as to what is meant by sin. Do these teachers — and we who do not hold sinlessness to be a possible attainment — mean the same thing by the word sin? I answer confidently, that we do not, at least in the case of many of such teachers. They are wont to assume that sin is satisfactorily and sufficiently summarized as "the conscious transgression of a known law;" then, taking that as its sum and substance, they argue reasonably enough that a Christian may live for a length of time free from sin, i.e., not consciously transgressing a known law. But can we accept such a definition of sin? Must we not necessarily extend the idea of sin to a far wider circuit? Is it sufficiently defined by any narrower explanation than this: sin is anything and everything in man that is not in perfect accord with the holy will of God? The perfect will of God is the only ultimate standard of right and wrong; whatever comes short of that is not absolutely right, and, therefore, is of the nature of sin.

No man here on earth knows in its fullness what that will is, and, therefore, none may rightly assume that he is in perfect agreement with it. All who insist on the more limited definition of sin would probably allow that this wider definition excludes the attainment of sinlessness. Agreement in definition implies similarity of conclusions. It is not purposed to take up these questions about personal consecration one by one and use them as topics for successive chapters. Either will the positive instructions given in Scripture be studied, and incidentally these questions will find their solution. A little trouble devoted to apprehending the purpose and object of our Lord's instructions will produce a far more satisfactory conviction as to the meaning of personal consecration than the attempt to find a logical answer to a series of questions, however clearly this might be attained.

The subject itself, though but a branch of the greater topic of holiness, is an important element in that topic. Let the reader remember that the limits for consideration are fixed by the title of this book. The wider matter of holiness, and its subdivisions of power, purity, service, the work and fullness of the Holy Ghost, are not here under consideration. One thing alone is to concern us: what does our Lord teach, what do His apostles mean, about personal consecration? In the wider range of the call to holiness we find one portion of the subject occupied with this idea of personal consecration; just as in the whole book of Leviticus, entirely concerned with God's call to and provision for holiness, there is one chapter exclusively relating to the consecration of the priests (Lev. 8). That chapter, with the parallel chapter in Exodus 29, provides the fullest exhibition of what our topic means.

Aaron and his sons had been called to the priesthood; and in order effectively to enter upon the office, they must pass through the act of consecration, or as some have suggested, the "filling the hands." In doing this, they placed certain portions of the sacrifice, together with some of the meal offering, upon their outspread hands. These representative gifts, the shoulder, the fat, and the bread, were then waved before the Lord for a wave-offering; and as such were finally burnt upon the altar. This act gives a vivid illustration of what the Scripture means by personal consecration. When actually carried out, it implies that the powers of the body, the affections of the heart, and the possessions of the offerer, are put in the hands, held out before God as an offering, taken over and accepted by Him. This "filling of the hands" leaves practically nothing over, that is not included in the presentation to God. All is the Lord's, by the deliberate gift of the soul, and by His acceptance of the gift.

If further emphasis is sought from the added word "personal," we take it to represent: first, the individual action of the soul, that each separate person for himself is called upon thus to consecrate himself to God; and next, that it is his whole person, the man and all that he is, which is to be the substance of the consecration.

His own hands are to be filled with the offering; the powers, affections and possessions which sum up himself and all he owns, are to be the substance filling his hands; and all these, himself in its fullest sense, are to be the individual offering, which he makes to God. It needs but a few words to show that this Old Testament picture is an intended reality for New Testament saints. For, in the first place, the title given to Aaron and his sons is applied to every Christian in the new dispensation. "Ye also, as lively stones, are built up a spiritual house, an holy priesthood"; "Ye *are*... a royal priesthood"; "and hath made us kings and priests unto God and his Father" (1 Pet. 2:5, 9; Rev. 1:6). Such is the definition of the calling given to every soul that has come to Christ (1 Pet. 2:4), and is washed from its sins (Rev. 1:5). The implied result of personal consecration is commanded further in direct language by Paul: "I beseech you therefore, brethren, by the mercies of God, that ye present your bodies a living sacrifice, holy, acceptable unto God..." (Rom. 12:1). And the same apostle assumes that the Corinthian Christians recognize themselves to be thus consecrated and belonging to God, when he says: "Ye are not your own? For ye are bought with a price: therefore glorify God in your body, and in your spirit, which are God's" (1 Cor. 6:19, 20).

9

Personal Consecration

Thus in faint outline, the idea of personal consecration lies before us: sufficient to show at the outset what a heart-searching thing it is, with what far-reaching results it is connected.

The phrase is perhaps lightly used, and the claim to the knowledge of it easily made. But where it is a real fact, and not a mere phrase, the effect must be enormous in the life. It goes as deep as the heart's affections, spreads as wide as the whole being, rises as high as the mind can reach, lasts as long as life itself. It is a tremendous upheaval in the existence where it is first consciously and thoroughly carried out; for it means the entire transference of rule, choice, decision and selection in life from self to God. It means the enrollment of the soldier, who will henceforth obey only one voice; the engagement of the servant to recognize only the master's will; the marriage of the bride, who leaves her own in order to share her husband's home. It means much of what man naturally shrinks from, "giving up;" but lest that thought should be a hindrance, let it never be forgotten how much it also means of the happy counterpart, "getting in exchange."

Amid the immense energy of the churches of Christ today, in many fields of active service, it may still be doubted whether there is any general or common and wide apprehension on the part of Christians, of their calling and life as "priests unto God." The closer nearness to God, the prevailing intercession with Him, the more intimate knowledge of His will, the clearer vision of His glory, the true representation of His character, the commission to reveal His mind: these were some of the peculiar functions and happy privileges of the true priests of God in old time. Many a true heart longs to know and exercise the like calling today, and yet is consciously far short of it. Does the hindrance lie here: that now, as of old, the priestly functions could never be lawfully exercised until the priestly consecration had gone before; and perhaps, the lack of the latter explains defect in the former? The following pages are a simple endeavor to trace out the sense, in which personal consecration is intended to be practiced in Christian lives.

First, a plain example of one in whom it was vividly exercised may serve to show the model for our imitation. Then the separate instructions of our

Lord, by which He taught the practical outcome of it all in daily life, will be examined closely, and their practical meaning sought. In the closing pages, the natural consequence is pointed out, by which the reality of the consecration is tested, and its existence in the individual life may be discerned and evidenced.

There is a large portion of God's promised blessings as yet unclaimed by the Church of Christ; and the door that leads in to them is labeled personal consecration. Some things have to be left behind by each soul who means to enter; but far grander things lie waiting to be possessed on the inner side. We may well say of this good land, what Pharaoh said of rich Egypt in comparison with famine-stricken Canaan: "Also regard not your stuff; for the good of all the land of Egypt *is* yours" (Gen. 45:20).

As the pages are read, may the reader's heart be led to a growing conviction of what personal consecration means, and a final decision to respond to the call, which was given in the words of David to Israel: "And who *then* is willing to consecrate his service this day unto the LORD?" (1 Chron. 29:5).

Chapter 2
A Typical Life

"A pattern to them which should hereafter believe on Him to life everlasting."
(I Timothy 1:16)

THE first two recorded utterances of the Apostle Paul represent the normal attitude of the soul, in the separate crises of conversion and consecration. "Who art thou, Lord?" This is at once a confession of the divine nature of the Saviour, and an inquiry as to how He may be known. The confession is a proof of the Holy Spirit's teaching: for "no man can say that Jesus is the Lord, but by the Holy Ghost" (1 Cor. 12:3); and the inquiry is that honest seeking, which has the promise that it shall find, and is the sure precursor of true conversion. "Lord, what wilt thou have me to do?" No sooner has the first question been answered, than this second one is uttered; which compresses into a single sentence the very essence of personal consecration. For wherever this question is put to the Lord, with a real desire to know and a heart purpose to carry out the answer, there consecration takes a practical start in the life.

In looking at these two questions, we gain authority for taking them as applicable to ourselves, and representative of a normal experience in Christians, by remembering that the apostle is a divinely given type for all believers (1 Tim. 1:16). As such, his various steps in the knowledge of Christ will serve as models to point out the pathway, along which other Christian lives will be developed. The fact that these two sentences were uttered in the same minute, by one whom we are thus warranted in regarding as a pattern for Christians, provides at once an answer to one of the moot questions about consecration. Must the experience of consecration be separated from that of conversion by a length of time, more or less extended? The example of the apostle is proof that there is no inherent necessity for such separation. The sudden illumination of the soul with the saving knowledge of Christ may instantly be followed by the recognition of His claim to the soul's consecration, and a loyal surrender to that claim there and then. There is no logical or essential necessity for a long separation between the two. But at the same time it must not be forgotten, that there was in the Apostle Paul a remarkable preparedness of soul, a pre-existing thoroughness of zeal for God and energy of religious life, which will largely account for the instant promptness, with which he grasped the meaning of Christ's call. In many other cases, where there was not before conversion this thorough earnestness, this heart purpose about God and His service, there may well be an interval of time sundering more or less widely the stages of conversion and of consecration.

Israel's story is also typical for Christians (1 Cor. 10); and from that we can see how the period of eighteen months, which intervened between the Red Sea and Kadesh Barnea, may represent the more normal experience of the mass of Christians. Whilst here and there some heart of courage, not to be dismayed by an early sight of war, may be able to take the direct route into Canaan, and enter it in three days; others, and those representing the majority of experiences, may need eighteen months to learn the same lesson and reach the same point.

Certainly Paul, at the end of three days, knew the answer to his question of consecration, and his example may surely be reproduced in other souls. But as certainly, Israel required an interval to reach the parallel point; and so may others to day. We conclude, therefore, that in this question of the relation in time between conversion and consecration, there is no need to insist either on a simultaneous or on a separated experience. Either may be true. The essential point for all to know is that the two facts exist, whenever they came about.

William Gurnall put the case, as to whether conversion must be sudden or might be gradual, with transparent clearness, when he wrote in effect: "There be many days when thou dost not see the sun rising, but thou knowest well when it is up." Sometimes the first ray is seen as it springs from the horizon, and at others a cloudy sky conceals altogether the moment of the sun's appearing. So upon some souls, as upon the jailer of Philippi, the light dawns in an instant; whilst upon others, as upon Nicodemus, the light breaks very gradually through the haze, and it is high morn before the full conviction of sunrise has impressed the soul.

Consecration runs on parallel lines with conversion, each alike is a question of soul-dealing with God; each concerns a gift and its transference from giver to receiver; each is a matter of faith in the soul concerned; each is a transaction intended to have a life-long consequence, and to be an irreversible step. Applying Gurnall's theory or illustration to consecration, it is possible to gradually recognize God's claim upon us, that only one by one are the different parts of life and being yielded to His rule and command. And again it is possible to see the demand at a single glance, and to respond in full purpose at once: "What wilt thou have me to do?" The crucial point, the urgent need for every true Christian is this: Whether gradually or suddenly, whether in a moment or after years, it matters not; but is your life now yielded to God, does it supply in practical obedience the answer to "What wilt thou have me to do?"

If Paul is indeed a type for "all who shall hereafter believe in Christ unto eternal life," then will the questions he uttered correspond to our experience, but the answers he received must guide our conduct. The answer to his question of consecration is summed up in the words: "For thou shalt be his witness unto all men…" (Acts 22:15). All else of his consecrated life is contained practically in that one fact, that he was a witness unto Christ. That governed his conduct, inspired his language, guided his steps, occupied his lifetime. And nothing less than that will reproduce in our lives the real essence of consecration. To be only and always a witness unto Christ, leaves no part of the being untouched by the claim of God.

His own language explains how in the apostle's case, this one call became his life's occupation: "…immediately I conferred not with flesh and blood…" (Gal. 1:16); at once all other influences and governing forces lost their power, God's voice alone must guide and determine his course. "…*other* lords beside thee have had dominion over us…" (Isa. 26:13): that was the past life; "*but* by thee only will we make mention of thy name" (viz., as Lord and Master): — that describes the future life of the consecrated soul. Again he writes: "I live, yet not I, but Christ liveth in me." And yet again: "To me to live *is* Christ…" Is it any wonder that so grand and far-reaching a testimony should follow, when so thorough a consecration went before? It is a great advantage for any soul, that would make the most of its life for God, when it comes as soon as may be from the reception of God's gift in conversion to this surrender of the answering gift in consecration. Alas! that many who have readily and thankfully followed this model man in the former, seem content to leave the model unnoticed in the latter.

It strikes us as a very bold, almost a presumptuous thing, to read the words: "Be ye followers of me, even as I also *am* of Christ" It has been called a mark of the self-conscious stage of his life, that the apostle could write these words; and a supposed early period of his soul growth, which he left behind at a later date. Yet if in all reality his life was devoted to the one purpose of being a witness to Christ, with no conscious reserve and no divided allegiance, then that sentence should rather be taken as a fresh item of testimony — a bold and a potent one — of what can be done when "not I, but the grace of God which was with me," is the power that lies behind the testimony.

This answer to his question, that he was to be a witness unto Christ, implies in itself the many things so frequently named as steps or aspects of the subject of consecration. To be a witness, always ready and prepared to give the needed testimony, must surely mean a surrender of time, of will, of power, yes, and of self, unto Him who demands the testimony. It is such a far-reaching demand, such a life-absorbing call, that when fairly and fully accepted, there is no part of the man left untouched thereby.

The apostle is really repeating the same call to Christians, to be followers of his example, and is only using another expression for it, when he writes to the Romans thus: "I beseech you therefore, brethren, by the mercies of God, that ye present your bodies a living sacrifice, holy, acceptable unto God, *which is* your reasonable service" (Rom. 12:1). Every word in that appeal has its own special bearing upon the subject of personal conse-cration. "I beseech you," as introducing the appeal, calls for a personal response, and makes it a matter for personal decision. As in an earlier stage, the soul is addressed: "As though God did beseech *you* by us: we pray *you* in Christ's stead, be ye reconciled to God" (2 Cor. 5:20); so now the already reconciled soul is called upon for a parallel of further decision. Everyone who recognizes that the response to the appeal for reconciliation constitutes the essence of conversion should also see in the response to this second appeal the essence of consecration. The two are, therefore, not of necessity so joined together, that the converted soul is also consecrated. No, there is a second appeal, demanding a second response, and develop-ing a second stage of the Christian life.

"Brethren, by the mercies of God." These words limit the appeal to those who are already members of God's household — brethren in His family, and conscious partakers of His mercy. Consecration is a lesson for those who have some preceding knowledge of God, and that especially in the way of mercies accepted, believed in and experienced. It is not and cannot be made, the first step of the Christian life. There is no ground for the appeal, and there will not be the right power for the response of consecration, unless there goes before the conscious reception of God's mercies — when, "according to his mercy he saved us, by the washing of regeneration, and renewing of the Holy Ghost." This is a matter of no small importance, in days when the appeal to live out the nobleness of a consecrated life is sometimes uttered and pressed upon those who have never yet been fitted for it by the preceding mercies of the washing and the renewing.

"That ye present your bodies a living sacrifice."

Here are three more of the elementary principles of consecration. First comes the idea conveyed by the word "present," that consecration is a defi-nite act. Something done, and done once for all, inasmuch as the very idea of presenting, giving, handing over, yielding up, implies the transference of a thing from one person to another, the imparting of a gift; that also enforces the same aspect of consecration as an act: for it is not conceivable that a gift can be gradually, slowly given. If it is a gift in reality, there must be a moment in which its transference takes place, logically speaking.

Next comes the subject of the gift, "your bodies." By so defining the matter with which consecration is concerned, the apostle makes it eminently practical, and removes the thought from the region of mere emotion, or even of the inner being alone. No, the body of the believer is to be the gift presented; and thereby, the whole man is included. With the body, if wholly given to God, there must also go its indwelling spirit and personal soul, its mental powers and warm affections and emotions, its outward possessions and belongings also. To name the body is most practically to include the whole man. He who in this sense presents his body to God, leaves nothing that is his unyielded or reserved for self. Thirdly, defining the gift as "living," there is probably a contrast intended between this sacrifice and the typical offerings of the Mosaic dispensation. Those, though brought before God and presented alive, were destined to immediate death; but this is purposed for a nobler end, that the body, in all its living powers, shall be owned by and used for God: that over the whole man there may be written the motto, "To me to live is Christ."

The word "sacrifice" denotes the holy purpose to which this life is to be devoted, as an offering to God. "Holy, acceptable unto God, *which is* your reasonable service." Here are three more marks attached to personal consecration, in what may be called its inward, upward and outward relations.

In the first place, it is defined as "holy." This is not a demand from which an honest soul may shrink back and say, "I am not holy, and so am unfit to make the offering." But it is a divine blessing attached inalienably to a true offering. For of old, when an Israelite brought his offering to God, and said in the words of the Psalmist: "... bind the sacrifice with cords, *even* unto the horns of the altar" (Ps. 118:27), the immediate result was that the offering became holy. For the law was clear upon this point: "Whatsoever toucheth the altar shall be holy" (Exod. 29:37). Contact with the altar constituted this holiness, in its prime sense of "separation unto God." So upon the willing presentation of the body to God, as it is yielded in obedience to God's will, it becomes at once a thing appropriated to God's use — i.e., holy.

We have not, therefore, to look for a certain amount or condition of intrinsic goodness, which is to constitute the holiness of our consecration; but we are to know, that upon the willing consecration of the body, God puts His mark of ownership, calls and recognizes it as His; and so it is holy. As such we are intended henceforth to treat it, and to act and live on the understanding, that "ye are not your own, ye are bought with a price."

Following this inward result of consecration there comes next the upward or Godward result: "acceptable unto GOD." Here is an answer to the question that often troubles honest hearts, whether their lives are actually well-pleasing to God. The first factor for such a life lies in this personal consecration. It forms a distinguishing mark between the forced service of an unwilling bond-slave, and the willing devotion of a loving servant: it means that "goodwill" in service, which gives it a welcome and counterbalances all other deficiencies.

It is a grand thing to know that God is willing to be pleased with us; and it should give a delight to this call to personal consecration beyond all else, that it puts us in a condition and relation to God corresponding to, although far short of, that of our blessed Lord, when the Father said: "This is my beloved Son, in whom I am well pleased."

The third result of such consecration is its outward bearing, its logical aspect before the world: namely, that it "is your reasonable service." The world which knows not God finds, alas, its strongest arguments against Christianity from the faulty conduct of professed Christians. It sees very keenly what ought to be the marks of a Christian life; it expects very logically that conduct shall correspond with profession, and the Christian be like Christ.

Every professed Christian puts forth the claim that he has been redeemed by and belongs to Christ. Then can you call it anything else but the natural consequence, that the Lord should possess and use what He has redeemed and acquired? In other words, personal consecration is only the honest surrender of the purchase to the purchaser; it is like sending home to the buyer what he has bought and paid for. It ought to be absolutely universal as the conscious act and condition of every Christian. It accords with reason, even in a worldly mind; it brings with it well-pleasing in the eyes of God; it affixes the true mark of holiness on the life of the one who has it.

At the same time it should be plainly understood, that such personal consecration, such a response to the apostolic appeal, such a following of the apostolic example, implies no claim whatever to a condition of sinlessness.

There is a world of difference between a surly, unwilling child, who never obeys his father save under compulsion, and a glad, loving, devoted child, who wants always to please his father. That difference corresponds to the change between the slow, hard service of an unwilling Christian, and the glad, willing life of one truly consecrated to the Master. But in the willing child's life, as in the consecrated soul's, there is yet the certainty of many a failure and many a fault, acknowledged and confessed when discovered, and amended and forsaken for the future; yet there, and known to be there, as growing light and knowledge reveal ever-widening vistas of the good and perfect and acceptable will of God.

We may sum up from the example and teaching of Paul certain definite conclusions as to personal consecration:

1. There need not be necessarily an interval of time between the conscious experiences of conversion and consecration.
2. But there may be such an interval, and in normal conditions there probably will be.
3. The question of the time when such conscious consecration comes about is quite unimportant; the crucial question is, whether the fact of it exists.
4. The essential outcome of personal consecration is a life of witness-bearing unto Christ.

5. Personal consecration is the subject of a personal appeal to Christians, and demands a personal response.

6. It is a definite act, as dealing with a gift.

7. It deals with the body, as including the whole man.

8. It issues in a life-long condition, consequent upon the act of giving.

9. It imparts holiness to the giver, good pleasure to God, evidence to the world.

10. It does not imply, and justifies no claim to, a condition of sinlessness.

Chapter 3
Christ As Master

"Ye call Me Master and Lord: and ye say well; for so I am."
(John 13:13)

THE underlying foundation for every call to a definite step in the Christian life must be the plain teaching of our Lord Himself. "What is written in the law? how readest thou?" That should ever be the final appeal of the teacher, who would enforce his lesson with authority; that should be the constant question of the disciple, who would make sure of right instruction. Only where the full Scriptures — in text and context, in main drift and particular expression — are studied and obeyed, will the student know with assurance what may be expounded as true, expected as possible and experienced as real, according to the mind of God.

"A Saviour, which is Christ the Lord." So ran the first message about Jesus to the shepherds, and such is ever the first heralding of the gospel to mankind. But that phrase is often sadly limited and curtailed in the reception, which men give to it, as though it meant only a Saviour from the guilt and final penalty of sin; as if nothing more than pardon for past sins and an escape from eternal punishment were comprised in Christ's salvation. There is no such limitation in the Bible. Judged by the Scriptures, it is a poor and pitiful form of the gospel, a dwarfed and contracted explanation of what we have in the "Saviour, which is Christ," when it is confined to this forgiveness of past sins, deliverance from hell and heaven gained at last. Used indeed as the mere beginning of the gospel, we say to such a definition: Yes, that is true. As a necessary starting point in the saved life: Yes, again. As the first syllable of salvation's meaning: Yes, once more. But when these three items are taken to be the sum and substance of the gospel, practically the whole of salvation in Christ, then we say emphatically: No, by no means. "A Saviour, which is Christ," has far more than that, in His name and His gospel. The very title of "Saviour" suggests a series of questions: What from? What for? At what cost? To what end? With what object? For what purpose? And only a full answer to these questions will give an adequate definition, or show the true limits of the salvation of Christ given unto men.

It is surely a poor thing on our part to take such a gift as this without a thought about the purpose of the Giver, and the result He aimed at and counted worth the infinite cost which He paid for it. It should be our response to seek eagerly what He desires from us, and what we may render as proof of our gratitude. And such a search will find its answer from the very title of "Saviour," and what it implies. As we ask what He is a Saviour from, we find that His is a deliverance from the guilt of sin, so that believers are justified (Acts 13:39); from the future penalty of sin, so that they shall not come into condemnation (John 5:24); from the dominion of sin, so that they should not serve it, but be free from it (Rom. 6:6, 12, 14, 22); from the bondage of Satan and the fear of death (Heb. 2:14, 15); from the yoke of the law and the lust of the flesh (Gal. 5:1, 17). If we ask again what He thus saves men for, we find it summed up in a sentence thus: That we "might serve him without fear, In holiness and righteousness before him, all the days of our life" (Luke 1:74, 75). A life of service, fearlessly and happily rendered; with a heart that belongs to Him, and conduct that glorifies Him; lived out in His conscious presence, and lasting to our last day on earth: that is the purpose He has for His people, that is the aim of His salvation, which must be ours if we would satisfy His heart, and fulfill His good will for us.

Taking one of the four Gospels to illustrate His teaching, we will notice how the earlier chapters of Matthew bear upon our subject, and serve to enforce the demand for personal consecration by the very words of our Lord Himself. To begin with, it is remarkable that the topic of His earliest preaching (4:17), as of His forerunner the Baptist's message (3:2), of the first commission to the twelve (10:7), and of the second commission to the seventy, was "the kingdom of God" (Luke 10:9), "the gospel of the kingdom" (Matt. 4:23).

The parallel records in Mark and Luke substitute the phrase, "the kingdom of God," which has erroneously been supposed to indicate some other message. That the phrases are meant to be identical may be seen by comparing Matthew 10:7; Luke 9:2; and Matthew 4:17; Mark 1:15; and Matthew 13:31; Mark 4:30; where the two phrases are used interchangeably. In fact, the similarity of our modern language, when we speak alike of the British dominions, or the dominions of the queen, serves to show that these are but two expressions of the same thing: the divine rule among men.

Too little emphasis has been given amongst the churches of Christ, to this aspect of the gospel as revealing a kingdom. If it is a kingdom, there must be over it a king: and by the title of king there is implied rule, authority, government, dominion on His side; submission, obedience, service and subordination on ours.

Presently, in this same Gospel, there follows the enunciation of the laws of this kingdom, which we call "the Sermon on the Mount." Selecting from it two sentences for our present purpose, we read in Matthew 5:44, 45: "But I say unto you, Love your enemies, bless them that curse you, do good to them that hate you, and pray for them which despitefully use you, and persecute you; That ye may be the children of your Father which is in heaven ... " Honestly and deliberately considered, this is really a tremendous demand; one that implies for its obedience all that can be meant by personal consecration. Such a word, accepted by the hearer, can only be fulfilled where loyal devotion and heart-whole surrender of the whole being to God have put aside every earthly and natural tendency to repay evil with evil, and have enthroned God's will alone in their place. Think for a moment, whether obedience to this law of Christ is universal in the professing church, whether it is the habitual outcome of the gospel, whether it forms the usual distinguishing mark of God's children, whether (most important of all) it is the habitual practice of our own lives. Must we not sadly confess that it is not so; that this law seems to have been almost blotted out from the rules, which apparently guide the majority of Christians? And why is this so? What hinders those who call Christ their Saviour, from giving this evidence of their salvation? Probably this one reason: that so many Christians have ignored the call to personal consecration, which must underlie obedience to such a law.

Our second sentence from the Sermon on the Mount is Matthew 6:24: "No man can serve two masters..." That is a very natural and obvious statement, one that commends itself at once to every thinking mind. See then how our Lord applies it, in saying further: "Ye cannot serve God and mammon." His words do not admit of a third possibility, in which neither one nor the other is served. No, we must serve. *"Ich dien"* is the motto of every life; servants we are, the great question, on which hang the real issues of life, is: "Whom shall we serve?" The result in view is that a definite choice must be made; and by that choice the character of the life will be determined. Then, where the choice is rightly made, and the service deliberately entered, you have in its very essence what is meant by personal consecration. To halt between two opinions, to live a divided life, to yield a partial and wavering service, is a miserable experience, unsatisfactory alike to the servant and the master.

Again, in these earlier chapters of Matthew, we find that our Lord on three occasions issued the command: "Follow me." To Peter and Andrew, amid their daily avocation as fishermen (4:19), to the disciple, who wished first to go and bury his father (8:22); to Matthew, as he sat at his official post (9:9); came the authoritative call, that required an immediate decision and response. You will notice the autocracy, which such a call assumes; for the claims of a business calling, the ties of domestic life, and even the duties of a government official, are put aside in a moment by these men, when they hear and obey Christ. Surely, that is a plain illustration of personal consecration. There can be no doubt that such a call could only be obeyed where the life was surrendered, the will submitted, the heart yielded to the Lord. That these men did so obey and follow Christ, shows how they understood His claims upon them; and how His demands took first place, and all else second, in their lives. Nor must we put aside the point of the Saviour's call, by supposing that He may so call some, but not all, of His professed people. That we all owe Him service is a matter granted without controversy; and that service can only be rendered by obeying this call is equally clear, when we hear Him say: "If any man serve me, let him follow me" (John 12:26). The call to follow Him is, therefore, binding on all His servants, as the call to serve is on all His redeemed people. Thus, His demand, "Follow me," lays upon every professed child of God the call to personal consecration.

One more passage puts this call in yet another light, when we read in Matthew 11:28, 29: "Come unto me, all *ye* that labour and are heavy laden, and I will give you rest. Take my yoke upon you, and learn of me..." Here is a double invitation and command. First, the familiar word of grace, in response to which our souls (if we are truly Christians) have come to rest on Him. About that we have no doubt; it was indeed a divine call to a divine blessing; and He has made the blessing true to everyone who has followed the call. But notice the second command. Immediately, without any apparent interval, at once after coming unto Him, there is heard the next step: "Take my yoke upon you, and learn of me." All who have found the rest from the fruitless toil and intolerable burden of sin by coming to Christ, are bidden at once to take the yoke of submission to Him and to sit at His feet as learners, disciples, scholars, under the Divine Teacher. Once more there is pressed upon us here the call to personal consecration: submission to another Master than self; entrance upon a life of learning, where the Teacher's will must be supreme and the Teacher's word our law. It is a school where only obedience can ensure knowledge: "If any man will do his will, he shall know of the doctrine..." (John 7:17); and where the humblest submission secures the highest attainments: "The meek will he guide in judgment, and the meek will he teach his way" (Ps. 25:9).

The above summary of the Lord's teaching surely suffices to produce deep conviction, that His purpose for all whom He has drawn near to Him and pardoned, and His claim upon them, is nothing less than absolute submission to His rule, surrender to His demands, service to His will. The very titles He assumes in these passages are enough to settle the matter. He is a King: and He can expect no less than His ancestor and prototype received, when "... all Israel obeyed him. And all the princes, and the mighty men, and all the sons likewise of king David, submitted themselves unto Solomon the king" (1 Chron. 29:23, 24). He is a Lawgiver, and he is a Leader:

27

so then there can be due to Him no less honour than was given by Israel to their lawgiver and their leader when they said: "All that thou commandest us we will do, and whithersoever thou sendest us, we will go According as we hearkened unto Moses in all things, so will we hearken unto thee…" (Josh. 1:16, 17). He is a Ruler or Lord with a yoke of dominion, real though easy to be borne; and He is a Teacher, with authority over His scholars and a task to appoint them, though it be light for meek and lowly learners. Then He may well say to us, as to His disciples: "Ye call me Master and Lord; and ye say well, for *so* I am … I have given you an example, that ye should do as I have done to you… If ye know these things, happy are ye if ye do them" (John 13:13, 15, 17).

The whole principle of the subject under consideration is conveyed in a single sentence, the importance of which may be judged by its sevenfold repetition in God's name to Pharaoh, and its fitness for our own use proved by the fact that Israel's circumstances were typical of ours (1 Cor. 10:11): "Let my people go, that they may serve me" (Exod. 13:1). "Let my people go" speaks of deliverance from bondage, escape from judgment, ease from burdens, freedom from oppression and cruelty and slavery, which had been Israel's lot in Egypt. That speaks to us also of a far wider deliverance, a more wonderful escape, a deeper rest, a grander freedom, in which the soul is ransomed from the power of Satan and the bondage of sin. Almost every soul that has come to Christ and found this deliverance can see in Israel's escape the picture of their own, and can trace at once their divine parallel to the Lamb, the Blood, the Cloud, the Rock, the Manna, and the God-given Leader. See now what was for Israel the divine aim and purpose of this deliverance: why did the Lord command Pharaoh to let His people go? "That they may serve me." Not delivered, in order to do their own will; not escaped from Pharaoh's rule, that they might be their own masters; not freed, with a view, henceforth, of following their own bent and finding a self-chosen path. No, that might have been possible had the deliverance been of their own accomplishing, if their own arm had conquered Pharaoh, and their own power gained them liberty. But mark well, it was a liberty and deliverance gained by a ransom price, a redemption purchase, a divine interference, a Saviour God. Then He who saved and purchased had a right to the disposal of His property; He who led captive the conqueror had the sole claim to the spoil; He, who ransomed the slaves had the appointment of their future. And He did this in a word: "that they may serve me." There was the life-call for Israel, the only but most blessed alternative to Egyptian bondage; that was God's object in effecting their deliverance, His purpose for their future: "that they may serve me."

For us who are Israel's anti-type; for us, who know a grander redemption from a deeper bondage at a far more awful price than they ever knew; for us, who were once Satan's "goods" (possessions), but are now Christ's "spoils" (Luke 11:21, 22); yes, for us, too, there is no other purpose in all this grace unspeakable, but one: "…that we, being delivered … might serve him …" The deliverance was effected by payment of a price, thereby constituting the delivered ones to be purchased possessions. The purchaser has, therefore, the right of control over the purchase; and He demands its exercise to the full: "Ye are not your own? For ye are bought with a price: therefore glorify God in your body, and in your spirit, which are God's" (1 Cor. 6:19, 20).

The teaching of our Lord, and the outcome of the salvation which He expects and demands, are thus put beyond dispute. Personal consecration is the natural result, the obvious fruit, the logical end of pardon imparted and acceptance granted by God, through the death and resurrection of Jesus Christ. No one who recognizes the cost at which these blessings were obtained, and the principle on which they were given, can have a doubt as to what the issue ought to be in the lives which enjoy these gifts. It becomes a mere matter of honesty, that which belongs to the Lord by right of purchase, should be yielded up to Him by the willing choice and deliberate surrender of the purchased possession. The matter was practically illustrated once by Pastor Theodore Monod under the following figure: "A man is passing out of a hall, and sees someone in front of him drop a piece of paper. He picks it up and discovers that it is a five-pound note. He hesitates a moment as to how he shall deal with it, and then says: 'I will give that man who dropped it one pound, and I will keep four.' But of course his conscience interposes, and tells him that that will not do. 'Well,' he resumes in thought, 'I will give him four, and only keep one pound.' Conscience objects again and insists on more than this. At last, with a sigh, the finder says: 'Then I will do a grand thing; I will consecrate the whole five pounds to the man who lost it.' But anyone who had heard his thoughts would say that it was no very grand thing after all, but a mere matter of ordinary honesty, to give the man what was his own."

The story fits well enough for the subject we have in view. In truth, the matter of personal consecration is reduced to the simple element of honesty. You have found yourself to be the ransomed and purchased possession of the Saviour; what then will you do with this treasure? Be honest, and you can only do one thing: give the possession to Him who purchased it, and treat it henceforth as His, not yours.

Beyond this first principle of the subject, there are, however, not a few details in the practical working of it. Our Lord does not leave us in uncertainty as to His meaning, but explains step by step how it must be developed in the daily life and conduct. His words apply the matter to the smallest details, and in the widest range of our being; and show how personal consecration bears on ourselves, our lives and homes, our surroundings and possessions, until nothing is left untouched by His all-embracing and all-absorbing claims. As we study these details, let it be with prayer that we may understand, and with practice that we may do them. "If ye know these things, happy are ye if ye do them."

A summary of our Lord's teaching from the earlier chapters of Matthew indicate, that He claims:

　　1. the position of a King, with absolute dominion over His people;
　　2. the character of Lawgiver, exacting obedience to His laws;
　　3. the place of a Master, with authority over His servants;
　　4. the title of Leader, exercising complete control over His followers;
　　5. the name of a Teacher, to whom His scholars owe entire submission.
　　6. Further, we conclude that all these titles and positions necessitate one and the same attitude towards Him on the part of His

people; that which we express concisely by the phrase, personal consecration.

7. Lastly, that this attitude ought to be the most natural and simple on the part of all who profess to be His disciples, being nothing more than the mere outcome of honest dealing: rendering unto God the things that are God's, yielding to Him and treating as His what He has made "his own possession."

Chapter 4
Discipleship

"... then are ye My disciples indeed."
(John 8:31)

IT was in the early days of the church that "the disciples were called Christians ..." (Acts 11:26): but in these later days, there is much need that the
Christians should come to be called disciples. For it seems to have passed
out of the ordinary estimate of Christianity, that "Christian" and "disciple"
are meant to be interchangeable terms; and that those who lay claim to the
former title should naturally vindicate their claim, by the witness of the
latter title as stamped upon their lives.

The steps by which these names became attached to the early believers
are plain enough. Men listened to the teaching and believed in the message
of the gospel; on profession of their belief, they and their households were
baptized in the name of Christ; and then as learners in His school, they
were at once called "disciples." Probably the constant use of the name of
Christ among disciples; their perpetual reference to that name in prayer
and praise, in preaching and converse; their appeal to that name as the title
of their Saviour, Guide, Ruler, Master, and Friend; caused them soon to be
known as Christ's men, and made it most natural that others should call
them "Christians." It is possible, however, that others outside the church
only adopted a name, which had been given to them by divine authority;
and that the title of Christian was affixed by God, and only then recognized
as fitting and brought into general use. This is the inference drawn from the
peculiar word translated "called" in Acts 11:26, for in every other passage
where it occurs in the New Testament, it is used of a divine communication
imparted to man. We may, therefore, with good show of reason assume
that it was a divinely-given title. But in any case, the special point to be
emphasized is this: that the title was only given and, strictly speaking, only
belongs to those who are actually "disciples" of Christ. It meant a good deal

for all who laid claim to it in those early days. To be a professed learner in His school, a proclaimer of His gospel, a follower in His steps, meant also to share His treatment at the hands of the world. Those who would be known by the name of Christian, were for three centuries at least liable at any time to be included in the fierce cry of the persecutors: "Christianas ad leones" — The Christians to the lions!

But for many long centuries, the title of Christian has become attached rather to countries, races and nations; and is no longer confined to its original and strict use, when only "the disciples were called Christians." The close connection intended between Christian and disciple has been overlooked; a formal, national, ecclesiastical, or functional meaning has been substituted for the original, primitive and Scriptural sense. It will be well for us all who desire to be known by the name of Christian, to trace it back to the fountain-head, to make sure of what the name means and entails, and to seek a practical evidence of that meaning in our own lives. There is no doubt that in apostolic days, "Christian" meant "disciple of Christ." Now let us find what is the exact definition of the name "disciple."

Taking the word disciple by itself, there is no question whatsoever that its meaning is "one who learns," "a learner," "a scholar," implying that all Christians were scholars in the school, and learners at the feet of Christ; and that those who went out to preach the gospel were to make "learners" of all who professed to receive the message.

When the early pages of the Gospel are studied, there appear three steps in the history of all those who became in this true sense "Christians." In the first place, they heard the call of Christ; next, in obedience to the call, they followed Christ; and then, as being under His teaching, they are immediately named "disciples" of Christ. See Matthew 4:18, 21; 5:1. Thenceforth, throughout this Gospel they are called disciples; varied only with the name "apostles" (that is, "sent ones"), on the occasion when they are first "sent forth" to preach the gospel (Matt. 10:2, 5). The former title, with which we are concerned now, expresses, therefore, the abiding relation of the followers of Christ to their Master. Whatever He may commission them to do, whatever character or calling He may impress upon them towards the world or the church, it remains the permanent condition between Christians and Christ, that the latter is Teacher and the former are disciples.

It is possible, of course, to use the word learner in a weak or loose sense, as of one who occasionally, intermittently, or somewhat indifferently studies a subject, but there is no such vague sense attached to the word disciple. Judging by those to whom it first belonged, it meant a continual following, a constant listening and consistent obeying on their part towards the Master. It was a lifelong business, and a life-absorbing occupation, to be a disciple of Christ; treading in His steps, growing in His likeness, doing His works, meeting with His treatment by the world, sharing His sufferings, and waiting for His glory.

There are three places in the Gospel according to John, where our Lord gives three great principles, which seem to embody and depict in the fullest sense the far-reaching and all-embracing idea of discipleship. In the midst of various objections made against Him by the Pharisees, and some vague questionings by other Jews, in John 8:30, we read: "As he spake these words, many believed on him." Apparently, they at once professed their belief and so separated themselves from the opposing Pharisees and the mere external listeners. But lest they should deceive themselves as to what belief in Christ meant, and what results it must have, He at once lays down the first of these principles of discipleship as follows: "Then said Jesus to those Jews which believed on him, If ye continue in my word, *then* are ye my disciples indeed; And ye shall know the truth, and the truth shall make you free" (John 8:31, 32). This first principle gives an inward view of discipleship, explains the relationship established between the disciples and the Teacher, and implies that without it, the discipleship is a merely nominal and not a real thing. With the principle laid down for observance, there is joined also a promise of a consequent blessing; cause and effect are represented by the two verses just quoted; the soul that abides in the word of Christ becomes assured of the truth, and possessed of the liberty, which the truth conveys.

"If ye continue in my word." In the 43rd verse, we read: "Why do ye not understand my speech? *even* because ye cannot hear my word." Here, "my word" is distinguished from "my speech;" the latter meaning the separate and individual utterance; the former, the whole substance and tenor of the teaching of the Lord. The verse may be paraphrased thus: "Why do you not understand the sentences I am speaking to you? Why do you not know the meaning of what I am now saying to you? Because your ears are closed to My teaching altogether; because your heart is not opened to welcome My message as a whole." This verse serves, therefore, to explain the principle of discipleship we are considering, and represents it as an abiding in the whole teaching of Christ. It is an "abiding," or continuing, because of the life-long character of discipleship: it begins with the first hearkening to and learning of the teaching; it develops into a perpetual study and a widening grasp of that teaching. Cease from the teaching and you cease from discipleship; the two are joined of God; if one is deserted, the other is lost. "My word" unveils the wide extent of study, which the school of Christ contains. Christ Himself is "The Word," the utterance of the Father by which He reveals His mind to man. Christ's teaching as a whole is called by Himself "My Word," by which He, in turn, reveals the Father unto men. "My Word" is the sum and substance of all that Christ expressed and uttered to mankind. It includes the teaching of the Old Testament, for "...beginning at Moses and all the prophets, he expounded unto them in all the scriptures the things concerning himself" (Luke 24:27). It comprises the whole of the Gospels, which are expressed as "... all that Jesus began both to do and to teach, Until the day in which he was taken up..." (Acts 1:1, 2). It embraces the rest of the New Testament, as we judge from the word "began" in Acts 1:1, which implies that He continued teaching through the apostles; and as is expressly stated in Revelation 22:16: "I Jesus have sent mine angel to testify unto you these things in the churches."

With this wide range of study, put before the disciples of Christ is joined the double blessing of a growing knowledge of the truth and a growing liberty thereby. It assures the one who is "truly" or "indeed" a disciple, that his abiding in the word of Christ will have constant encouragement attached to it. "The Truth," which is practically coextensive with "The Word," (for

Christ is known by both titles), shall become a conscious possession; and with the possession shall come the fruit of it — liberty. A glorious fruit, little known, rarely sought for, feebly desired, faintly understood; yet a part of the heritage of the church: "… the liberty wherewith Christ hath made us free" (Gal. 5:1).

The second principle of discipleship, as explained by the Master Himself, is found in John 13:34, 35: "A new commandment I give unto you, That ye love one another; as I have loved you, that ye also love one another. By this shall all *men* know that ye are my disciples, if ye have love one to another." As the first principle related to a condition prevailing between the disciple and the Master alone, so the second principle connects the Master and the disciple on the one hand, and each disciple with all his fellow disciples on the other. With regard to the Master, the second principle of discipleship is that of obedience to His commandment; and with regard to the fellow disciples, the principle works out in a reflection towards one another of the Master's love towards each.

"A new commandment I give unto you." It is natural enough that the learner should be subject to the Teacher's rules and orders. As the first principle related to the study of the Master's teaching, here, the second insists on obedience to the Master's commands. The one is as reasonable as the other; for a scholar can only profit from his teacher's instruction if he joins study and obedience together. But the special commands may differ with different teachers; and here, the one prime command in connection with discipleship is this: "That ye love one another; as I have loved you … that ye also love one another." It is a command joined immediately with an example; the Master practices what he preaches; the scholar is bidden to do both what he hears and what he sees. The command is simple enough; no one can misunderstand what it means; the perfect example of the Master makes it as plain to the eye, as His direct words make it to the ear. Yet as soon as we raise our eyes from the Model, and fix them on the copies, we are almost unable to recognize the likeness. Is it not proverbial that theological hatred is the fiercest of all; and are not the wranglings and quarrels of professed followers of the Master the readiest argument of the world against His service? If this be really a principle of discipleship, the grievous conviction rises upon our minds that the number of "disciples indeed" must be desperately few; or that they are, for the most part, in the lowest class, where the first lesson of obedience is still being learned, but has not yet been mastered.

Face this principle of discipleship honestly. Here is obedience commanded, and the law to be obeyed is delivered. Then let each one ask himself, What is my position with regard to it? Is this reflection of the Master's conduct apparent in my own life? Do I love fellow disciples as He loved me? And if not, am I a disciple at all? We may not push it off as a lesson for far-advanced disciples. It comes at the outset; it is the B of the gospel alphabet, as faith in Christ is the A. "This is his commandment (A), That we should believe on the name of his Son Jesus Christ, and (B) love one another, as he gave us commandment" (1 John 3:23). It is a lesson so important, that in the first epistle of John it is made a condition of abiding in the light (2:10), a ground of assurance of new life (3:14), a secret of answered prayer (3:22, 23), a proof of divine birth and divine knowledge (4:7), and a *sine gua non* for God's indwelling and His love being perfected in us (4:12).

A reward attaches to this second principle as to the first. The first concerned an inward relationship, and had an inward reward. This second concerns an external relationship, and has an external reward. "By this shall all *men* know that ye are my disciples, if ye have love one to another" (John 13:35). While discipleship is incipiently a private matter between the scholar and the Teacher, it must very soon become one of public evidence. Here again, there is a double blessing in the reward; like Abraham of old, the obedient disciple is blessed and is made a blessing: all men who behold him are constrained to attest and acknowledge his discipleship, the outward seal is added to the inward; and all men who behold him get an insight into the religion of Christ and the blessing it imparts, which cannot be gainsayed. Surely, here is a strong appeal to all who are called Christians. The Master's command is imperative; let us obey it. The condition of discipleship is unalterable; let us accept it. The rewards are worth having; let us win them.

The third principle of discipleship is thus expressed by the Master: "If ye abide in me, and my words abide in you, ye shall ask what ye will, and it shall be done unto you. Herein is my Father glorified, that ye bear much fruit; so shall ye be my disciples" (John 15:7, 8). Five items of spiritual life and character are here joined together: abiding in Christ, His words abiding in the believer, prevailing prayer, much fruitfulness, bringing glory to God. Attached to these items is the sentence that applies them to our subject: "So shall ye be my disciples." A little lower in the chapter we read another verse, which similarly joins two of these marks: "... I have chosen you, and ordained you, that ye should go and bring forth fruit, and *that* your fruit should remain: that whatsoever ye shall ask of the Father in my name, he may give it you" (John 15:16). We may conclude from this that fruitfulness in the Christian life is a principle of discipleship, and that the conditions under which alone it can exist are those of the context just quoted.

"That ye bear much fruit." Taking this to be an essential element of discipleship, we can at once perceive how naturally it follows upon the preceding principles. No scholar can continue persistently in his master's teaching, loyally obeying his rules and commands, without attaining the result aimed at by the master; that is, without producing the fruit intended by the instruction. So the inward principle of abiding in Christ's words, and the outward marks of obedience to Him, will surely result in the upward development of fruit to God's glory. The connection of the separate principles is apparent from our passage, in which regular steps of progress are noted. First comes "abiding in Christ," which is practically synonymous with obedience; for He says, "If ye keep my commandments, ye shall abide in my love ..." (verse 10): this is our second principle. Next follows "Christ's words abiding in the believer," which is the counterpart to "abiding in His word": Out of this comes a grand result of practical experience: "Ye shall ask what ye will, and it shall be done unto you." And on that condition it can easily be seen that "much fruit" will result.

Looking at this principle of discipleship, as here depicted, and then looking for its counterpart in the living church, serves but again to emphasize a sad contrast between the divine purpose and the human fulfillment. Not fruit only, but "much fruit," springing from prevailing prayer, and resulting in glory to God — that is our Lord's principle of discipleship. Little fruit, uncertain prayer, small glory to God, seem rather the marks of professing Christians today. Is it not so? I speak as to wise men, judge ye. In you, reader, is it much fruit, sure prayer, full glory to God? Well, if there was failure in the former principles, there must be failure here. Discipleship is a connected idea; it takes steady work and regular steps to make progress in this school. But it can be done, and it is for us to do it. Let us make of our discipleship a fact and not a name. Abiding in His word, we shall know what is possible for us according to His mind. Obedience to Him will bring with it a confidence in His power and support, and a courage to ask boldly and assuredly what He teaches. That means fruit, much fruit; and a deeper, yet more glorious seal, the very witness of God: "And ye shall be my disciples."

Again, it is worthwhile pondering the rewards attached to this principle. Upwards, it brings glory to God: and that is perhaps the highest goal that man can ever reach. Within, it attaches God's testimony to the soul, like that which He gave to Enoch (Heb. 11:5), of the reality and acceptance of the soul's discipleship. It is a beautiful climax that we have reached. The first principle gives personal assurance to the soul; the second imparts convincing proof to the world; the third brings glory to God.

In a brief summary we conclude:
1. that "Christian" and "disciple" ought to be manifestly combined titles for every believer;
2. that discipleship is in reality such an absorbing thing, that it demands personal consecration for its realization;
3. that our Lord attaches to discipleship three great principles, without which it is not a working reality;
4. that the first of these is permanent continuance in the Master's teaching;
5. that the second is obedience to the command, that disciples love one another;

6. that the third is much fruitfulness to God's glory, through prevailing prayer;

7. that to each principle particular rewards are attached, present results of blessing inseparable from discipleship.

Chapter 5
Following Christ

"If any *man* will come after Me."
(Matthew 16:21)

THE phrase "personal consecration" does not occur in the New Testament; but the preceding chapters have indicated how it contains in itself the very essence of discipleship. The connection between these two ideas is so close that the former is the only element in which the latter can exist, and the latter is the logical outcome inseparably bound up with the former. It is, therefore, true to say that the foundation principles of personal consecration are those which are found to underlie discipleship: namely, permanent continuance in the words of the Master, loyal obedience to the commands of the Master and large fruitfulness in the service of the Master.

A further step is taken, however, in the apprehension of what personal consecration means, when beyond these general principles there are also seen to be minute and particular statements as to the practice they involve. Besides the three main ideas, which were found to be expressed by our Lord and were examined in the last chapter, His words also convey very clear and distinct conditions, upon which these ideas are developed in the life and experience of His disciples. In other words, it may be said that when the principles of discipleship are accepted, there will still be needed further instruction, as to the conditions upon which they are practically developed in the life. A soldier who enlists, and is enrolled in the queen's army for a period of seven, fourteen, or twenty years, understands at the outset that he has to abide under the instructions, obey the commands, and carry out the service given by the officers set above him. His principles of service are exactly those of the disciple in the school of Christ. But under those principles he naturally expects very full instructions in detail, as to his training, drill, exercise, maneuvers, location, expeditions, food, uniform, housing, pay, rewards, restrictions and pension. Some of these are enrolled in fixed codes of instruction, and applicable to every soldier alike; others will vary according to the circumstances and requirements of different branches of the service, different regiments, and different positions occupied by the soldiers. In this sense it is quite a natural thing that we should look under the general principles of discipleship, for more particular details and conditions of its exercise.

Such details are given by our Lord, quite as distinctly and emphatically as are the main principles already considered. On three different occasions, in the story of the Gospels, our Lord gave, in slightly varying terms, the stringent and unvarying conditions upon which alone the principles of discipleship can be carried into practice. They are uttered with very deliberate emphasis, they are enforced with strong repetition, they are made of universal application, they are declared to be of unalterable character. They serve to paint in clear colors the true conditions, which are involved in the reality of personal consecration. It will be well to study them with the conviction impressed upon our minds and hearts, that these are the terms upon which alone our Lord makes discipleship possible, and these are the conditions which must be observed, where personal consecration is to be a reality in the life of the Christian.

The first occasion upon which these terms are unfolded occurs in the tenth chapter of Matthew, and they form part of the Master's instructions to His disciples, as He sends them forth on their first mission journey. He unfolds to them at length the full line of service they are to follow. He tells them where they are to go, what they are to do, how to behave, what to avoid and what to choose, what to expect of treatment from the world, what of hatred, persecution, punishment, betrayal they will meet with. In view of this description, which might well make the stoutest hearts quail, He bids them have no fear, to take Himself as example, to look for the coming time of judgment for the righting of all wrongs, to trust in God's care and to look for His reward. Then, as though to answer the unspoken questions of the heart, — who is sufficient for these things? how can such service be rendered ? — He gives the first statement of the conditions which must underlie such service, conditions of personal consecration, in these words: "He that loveth father or mother more than me is not worthy of me: and he that loveth son or daughter more than me is not worthy of me. And he that taketh not his cross, and followeth after me, is not worthy of me. He that findeth his life shall lose it: and he that loseth his life for my sake shall find it" (Matt. 10:37 – 39).

The second place where these conditions of discipleship are given follows immediately upon the first statement by our Lord of the suffering and death He must undergo at the hands of the Jews. Such words seemed so amazing to the disciples, such an end to so blessed a life as their Master's, so out of all ordinary reckoning, that Peter expresses probably the thoughts of them all, when he "…began to rebuke him, saying, Be it far from thee, Lord: this shall not be unto thee." Our Lord rebuked the rebuker; called him a stumbling block, a hindrance in the path appointed; declared that his thoughts were earthly and not divine; and then applied this demand for surrender to God's will, and obedient walking in His path, even if it meant reproach, suffering and death to all disciples, in these words: "Then said Jesus unto his disciples, If any *man* will come after me, let him deny himself, take up his cross, and follow me. For whosoever will save his life shall lose it: and whosoever will lose his life for my sake shall find it. For what is a man profited, if he shall gain the whole world and lose his own soul? or what shall a man give in exchange for his soul?" (Matt. 16:21 – 26). The same story is told, in almost the same words, both by Mark (8:31 – 37), and Luke (9:22 – 25); and in all three reports it is followed by a warning to those who fail thus to follow, and who are ashamed of Christ; and that warning is followed by the story of the Transfiguration.

The third description of the conditions of discipleship is found in the fourteenth chapter of Luke. It is given next in order to the parable of the great supper, and is followed in turn by the parables of chapter fifteen — the lost sheep, the lost coin and the lost son. The context thus lends special force to these conditions. It is as though the boundless freeness of the gospel, as shown in the parable of the supper, and the infinite love of God unfolded in the following three parables, required to be guarded from misuse. Nothing may be detracted from the grace and goodness of God therein revealed, but care must be taken to show what effect they must have in the recipients. No one must be allowed to deceive himself, and say, "I have received the gospel, I believe in God's love, it is all right with my soul, and now my life does not matter much." Between these parables, with all their grandeur of divine fullness and grace, there comes this sharp, solemn, incisive statement of what it means to have received the gospel; of what God intends to result from its reception; of what fruit in discipleship must follow real coming to Christ, being found of Him, returning to God. This then is the third statement of the conditions of discipleship: "If any *man* come to me, and hate not his father, and mother, and wife, and children, and brethren, and sisters, yea, and his own life also, he cannot be my disciple. And whosoever doth not bear his cross, and come after me, cannot be my disciple . . . So likewise, whosoever he be of you that forsaketh not all that he hath, he cannot be my disciple" (Luke 14:26–27, 33).

Thus, on three different occasions, to three different sets of people, and with a threefold repetition of phrases, or of their record, these lessons concerning the call to personal consecration are enforced. First to the twelve disciples (Matthew 10:1); then to the disciples and all the people (Mark 8:34; Luke 9:23); then to the great multitudes that followed Him (Luke 14:25), these conditions are addressed. In the first case, the phrase "not worthy of me" occurs three times; in the second, a threefold report of the occurrence is given us; in the third, the phrase "cannot be my disciple" is thrice uttered. It is hard to imagine how any form of teaching could have been adopted, that would more forcibly have impressed upon the hearers the importance, the necessity, the unalterable permanence of these conditions. Surely, our Lord meant His hearers to face the alternative, and make their choice, of accepting and obeying these conditions, or else of not venturing or presuming to call themselves disciples at all. Inasmuch then as His principles of dealing with men do not change, — He is the same yesterday, today, and forever — all the force and power of these conditions must refer to ourselves today. It was not for that time only, but for all time in the gospel dispensation, that these lessons apply; for having pressed them upon the disciples themselves, He sent them forth to "make disciples" (Matt. 28:19) of all nations, and, therefore, to lay down for these nations the rules made binding upon themselves.

It is worthwhile to pause before examining these conditions of discipleship one by one, to note more closely the three significant terms employed upon the three occasions quoted above. Attached to the conditions in the first passage is the thrice repeated phrase, "is not worthy of me." That appears as one of the consequences of rejecting His conditions; and the positive statement that one "is worthy of Christ" will be the consequence of accepting and obeying them. Here is one of the blessed fruits of discipleship and consecration that our Lord is pleased to impart: such a disciple is worthy of Him! A solemn possibility is presented: a soul may be called "worthy of Christ"; or, a soul may fail to be worthy of Him. The alternative will be decided for us individually, one by one, according as each submits to, or rejects, the Master's conditions of discipleship. It is interesting to trace from other passages how this worthiness is regarded as possible, is enforced as part of the Christian calling, and is connected with a life of consecration. It implies an acceptance of the gospel invitation at the outset (Matt. 22:8), whereby they are "worthy" guests. It is spoken of as a possible attainment that some shall be "accounted worthy to obtain that world, and the resurrection from the dead" (Luke 20:35). It is attached to watchfulness and perpetual prayer, as a result "… that ye may be accounted worthy to escape all these things that shall come to pass, and to stand before the Son of man" (Luke 21:36). It is an honor to the persecuted disciples, "… that they were counted worthy to suffer shame for his name" (Acts 5:41; cp. 2 Thess. 1:5). It is a frequent appeal to converts that they should walk "worthy of God and his calling" (Eph. 4:1; Phil. 1:27; Col. 1:10; 1 Thess. 2:12). Lastly, it is the description of what some faithful souls in Sardis should attain, "… which have not defiled their garments; and they shall walk with me in white: for they are worthy" (Rev. 3:4).

Prefixed to the threefold report of these conditions of discipleship, on the second occasion of their delivery, is the phrase: "If any man will come after me." If to be worthy of Christ is a result of obeying His conditions, a deliberate choice of Him as Leader is the introduction to that obedience.

Personal Consecration

It is not, therefore, by accident, unconsciously, at haphazard, with vaguely uncertain development, that this condition of consecration may be expected to appear in the life. It is a matter submitted to the choice, and determined by an act of the will, in a man. Taking the first disciples as an example, we find in their case a definite call to such a coming after Christ, followed by a decision of the will, and a fresh line of conduct adopted in the life (Matt. 4:19–22). They had heard about Him as Messiah, and acknowledged His claim as such, on an earlier occasion (John 1:40–42); so that they were already believers in Him. Then there came the call to come after Him; and it was their response to that call that constituted them actually disciples of Christ. The same strong expression of "willing" is connected with the first elements of the gospel life, when we read in Revelation 22:17: "Whosoever will, let him take the water of life freely;" and occurs again in John 7:17: "If any man will do his will, he shall know of the doctrine…" This latter is akin to the passage we are considering, and enforces the lesson that it is a definite action of the will that is called for, when the conditions of discipleship are to be accepted.

The third description of these conditions is connected with the three-fold repetition of the phrase, "He cannot be my disciple." Here is the very climax of the matter in the whole topic of personal consecration. Where this is not a reality, whatever else the soul may have, it cannot have effective discipleship. The repetition of the phrase is most marked. Conditions are ranged under three heads: touching the heart's affections, the life's conduct, the personal possessions; and then comes the demand for the consecration of these unto Christ, as the only way in which it is possible to be His disciple. Again, it passes the power of language to express with more of solemn emphasis, and of unmistakable clearness, what He laid down as the conditions, and how He meant them to be observed. There is great need to make much of this demand of our Lord. For in these days of much evangelistic fervor and success, there is frequent profession of faith in Christ, and acceptance of His free and full salvation, without apparently an equally clear grasp of what fruits must follow the profession, and what result is due from the acceptance. The story of the great supper is widely known and often used; the parables of Luke 15 are the very groundwork of gospel preaching. But are those who use them as careful to proclaim, and are those who receive the message as ready to accept, the Master's intermediate teaching, placed between these grand stories? Not for one moment would we limit the absolute freedom of the gospel offer of salvation, or curtail the infinite love of God that reaches down to our uttermost need. But dare we omit His own teaching as to the consequence of the salvation, and the purpose of that love, in the lives of those who welcome them. Great multitudes go with Him today, as they did then; publicans and sinners listen to His word of grace now, as of old. Then to all who listen and go with Him there should be given His own message, as to the call for the affection of the heart, the consecration of the life, the surrender of the possessions to Him, without which they "cannot be His disciples."

It is with the strongest conviction that this intervening message is much overlooked, that we press for a careful attention to its terms, a deliberate study of its meaning, and a personal decision as to its application, in each individual Christian. Think how much hangs in the balance! It is worthwhile to count the cost. It is no waste of time to come to a careful decision upon the matter, when our Lord attaches to it the high reward of being worthy of Him, the blessedness of a life of following Him, and the right to the title of a disciple of Christ. In the following pages, it is purposed to examine in detail the particular terms in which these conditions of discipleship are expressed, and the practical meaning therein of personal consecration. Several of these are commonly misunderstood, and their real meaning missed; others are ignored or passed over as apparently impracticable counsels of perfection; all are given but too little space in the usual routine of doctrine and practice of the Christian churches. In the order of the gospel pages, they will be seen to have a very wide bearing upon the life, so that really no part or portion of the human being is left untouched by the calls and claims of the Master. As they come before us one by one, we need to seek both the enlightenment of the heart to understand, and the preparedness of the heart to accept, what they mean in our own case and conduct. It must be, it ought to be, all or nothing. He who withheld not His own Son, but gave Him up for us all; He who gave His back to the smiters, and hid not His face from shame and spitting; He who loved not

His own life, but gave it up for us all — what can He ask that we should not be glad and delighted to give? Whatever He names as the proof of our gratitude for His love, of our faith in His truth, of our praise for His mercy, that we should delight to render to Him. Well, He has spoken and told us; He has left it plainly written, so that none need fail to grasp it. He wants worshippers, He calls for disciples, He desires followers in His footsteps, and reflections of His character. He tells us the terms on which we may give Him these things. What shall we say? What shall we do? Can we find a better response, a worthier reply than this: "All that thou commandest us we will do, and whithersoever thou sendest us we will go"?

In a brief summary of this chapter, it appears:

1. that under the general principles of discipleship and consecration we find particular details and conditions;

2. that these are expressed at length by our Lord on three separate occasions;

3. that they were addressed to disciples, the people generally, and to the multitudes who followed Him;

4. that they are connected with the three remarkable phrases of "being worthy of Christ," "coming after Christ," "being a disciple of Christ;"

5. that they are enforced either by a threefold repetition of the phrase, or a threefold record of its use; and

6. that the language employed is of such striking emphasis, and the conditions put in such a form and position, as to give them the highest place of importance in our Lord's teaching, and of esteem and attention in our own reception of them.

Chapter 6
The Affections Demanded

"He that loveth father or mother more than Me is not worthy of Me."
(Matthew 10:37)

IN the consecration of the priests, as described in Exodus 29 and Leviticus 8, we have noticed that three things were placed in their hands and waved before God. Of these three, the fat from around the heart and inwards of the offering represented the affections of the offerer; the right shoulder pictured the strength and powers of his body, the man himself; and the food from the basket stood for his goods and possessions. It was a typical representation of a man's response to God's call: "Thou shalt love the LORD thy God with all thine heart, and with all thy soul, and with all thy might" (Deut. 6:5). Now, in the New Testament description of the conditions of discipleship, we find the exact counterpart of these three offerings in Old Testament consecration. Corresponding to the fat of the heart — the love and affection offered there to God — we have here the call to love Him more than father or mother, more than son or daughter. Parallel to the right shoulder — the powers of the whole man, his very self there presented as an offering — we find here the call to deny himself and his own life for the Master's sake. Akin to the bread from the basket — the goods and possessions there held out for God's acceptance — we have here "all that the man hath" forsaken and given up for the Master's service. A more exact coincidence could hardly be demanded, in order to establish the position we have assumed, that discipleship is practically synonymous with personal consecration: the former cannot exist without the latter; it rests upon it and is bound up with it.

We are now in view of the Saviour's demand corresponding to the first of these three typical offerings. It is expressed in somewhat varying terms in the first and third of the three statements, in which the conditions of personal consecration are given. In Matthew 10:37, it runs thus: "He that loveth father or mother more than me is not worthy of Me: and he that loveth son or daughter more than me is not worthy of me." In the third passage, the terms are given in even stronger language, as we read in Luke 14:26: "If any *man* come to me, and hate not his father, and mother, and wife, and children, and brethren, and sisters… he cannot be my disciple." The repetition of the demand in this double form, the consequences of worthiness and discipleship depending upon it, the universality of its application to anyone who comes to Christ, give to these words an importance that cannot be exaggerated. Consider how it would sound and what it would mean in the ears of the first disciples; and then apply it for our own use and our own life today.

At the outset, we shall best guard against any misunderstanding of the words in Luke 14:26, by keeping them in close connection with the parallel passage in Matthew 10:37. Otherwise the words of "hating his father and mother" might cause needless offence or create a false impression as to the meaning of our Lord. That these words cannot mean hatred in the ordinary and bad sense of the word is evident enough from three considerations. First, our Lord came "not to destroy, but to fulfill" the law; and that law enjoined honor, obedience, and reverence towards father and mother (Matt. 5:17; Exod. 20:12; Lev. 19:3, Deut. 21:18). Then, in answer to the question of the rich young man, the Lord said: "If thou wilt enter into life, keep the commandments. He saith unto him, Which? Jesus said … Honour thy father and *thy* mother" (Matt. 19:17–19). And again, He rebuked the Pharisees for breach of this very commandment, when He said: "Why do ye also transgress the commandment of God by your tradition? For God commanded, saying, Honour thy father and mother…" (Matt. 15:3–6). It is not possible, therefore, that our Lord could have meant that His disciples were to hate their parents, in the evil sense of the word, since He so constantly referred to the fifth commandment as binding upon all men.

But there is a use of the word in our ordinary language, which both agrees with our Lord's expression here, and fits in exactly with His kindred description in Matthew 10:37. Suppose that one of two warm and intimate friends asked the other to do something for him, which the other for conscientious reasons had to refuse. We can well understand how the first of them might say: "Then what is your friendship worth? You don't really love me; you hate me." Neither of them would take the word hate in its absolute and evil sense, but it would quite naturally be taken in a relative sense, implying simply that someone or something else was loved better. The story is familiar to us, of one who was urged to avoid the perilous danger in the path of duty, and refused. Then when he was challenged as to the reality of his love, he answered:

> "I had not loved thee half so well,
> Loved I not honor more."

That is exactly the meaning of hatred in the text before us. Such hatred will mean a really ennobled love to those of earth's relatives nearest to the heart; it will be a truer, better, more perfect love, when the soul can say to them:

> "I had not loved you half so well,
> Loved I not Jesus more."

Such then being a quite natural use of the words "hate his father and mother," it corresponds simply enough with the other phrase: "He that loveth father and mother more than Me is not worthy of Me." It is a plain demand that the first place in the affections must be given to the Lord; that all demanded, other objects of love shall take the second place; that He alone is to sit on the throne of the heart; that in every question of rival claims and conflicting demands upon the heart, the verdict must be given in His favor. There is no doubtful tone about this call for the groundwork of consecration; the very best of the whole being, that without which all other gifts and service are valueless, the deepest love of the heart, is to yield its choicest wealth to Christ.

Does such a call sound hard to any who are listening, and asking what consecration really means? Is it more than seems fit or right, to displace father or mother, son or daughter, from the first position of the heart's love, in favor of another? Well, for an example of how it is rightly done apart from Christ, remember what an everyday occurrence it is for a loving and devoted daughter to forsake father and mother, and to give the first place in her heart to the husband of her choice. Do father and mother complain then? Nay, if they think the choice a worthy one, they are glad for their daughter, and readily consent to take the second place. What then if One who is beyond all others in worthiness, to whom the keen intelligences of heaven ascribe the sevenfold perfection of worthiness (Rev. 5:12), what if He appeals to the hearts He has redeemed to God by His blood, and puts in His claim for the first place in the ransomed heart's affections? Surely He is the one "whose right it is"; and the soul conscious of His grace, enlightened as to His love, knowing what He has done to prove it, must confess that He is worthy, must give Him what He asks: "My Son, give me thine heart…" (Prov. 23:26).

It is a wonderful thing, which no other religion in the world has dreamed of, that our God and Lord should want and should demand the love of His people. But so it is. Love ever wants love, and is not satisfied until it gets it. No other religion ever pictured the thought of a God who loved, and, therefore, could not imagine One who wanted love in return. Yet when the love in Him is understood, it is natural enough that the love to Him should be given. Look at the parables which follow in Luke upon this demand of the Lord from His disciples; they seem to explain why He should make and desire it. If any man should lose a sheep, he goes after and seeks it — why? Because he wants it: either the wool, or the flesh or the proceeds of its sale. But it is only because he wants it, that he troubles to seek and rejoices to find it. If any woman should lose a piece of money, she searches diligently for it — why? Because she wants it: whether for completing the ornamental headband (as perhaps in the parable), or for that which it will purchase and supply for her need. And if a loving father has lost a prodigal son, he grieves, and longs, and is not rested until the son is found — why? Because he wants him: to complete the family circle, to give him loving companionship, to satisfy his desire for heart affection and loving devotion. Yes, love wants love, and so the Lord desires and demands the first place in His disciples' heart. You look beneath the surface of this demand, and you find a new and wondrous revelation of what the Lord thinks of you, and why He asks you for this gift. It means that He prizes highly and finds His own joy in the affection of His people at its full. He deserves the best that they can give Him; and neither His heart nor ours will have their fullest satisfaction until He gets the response of true consecration, and we have learnt what it is in our deepest affections to "crown Him Lord of all."

The preaching of a partial gospel, in which the elements of repentance and faith are enforced to the exclusion of any reference to consecration and discipleship, has caused these latter topics to appear almost a new truth to many minds. To some even, because they appeared new, it has been a doubtful matter whether they are a true part of the gospel. Yet, taking the one condition of consecration referred to in this chapter — the Lord's demand for the first place in the affections of His people — how can that be called new, and how can it be doubted whether it is true, which from the first lines of the Mosaic covenant has been the continuous demand of God from His people? It needs but to be mentioned, and every reader of the Old Testament recalls at once, how frequently this call and claim of God is made. Take as an example the Book of Deuteronomy, in which the principles of the law are applied a second time, and with deeper emphasis, to God's people. There is found the passage quoted by our Lord as the first and great commandment: "Hear, O Israel: The LORD our God *is* one LORD: And thou shalt love the LORD thy God with all thine heart, and with all thy soul, and with all thy might" (Deut. 6:4, 5). From that central passage, there flows constant allusions to the same great demand and purpose of God; so that not less than twelve calls to the same blessed duty are found in this one book; and that the book to which all the other Old Testament writings refer as "the Law." (See Deut. 5:10; 7:9; 10:12; 11:1, 13, 22; 13:3; 19:9; 30:6, 16, 20).

In the pages of the Gospels, the call is not only enforced, but very directly obeyed and accepted by the disciples. When in Matthew 4:22, and in Mark 1:20, the Lord calls as disciples James and John, it is expressly stated: "They immediately left the ship and their father, and followed him;" "they left their father Zebedee in the ship with the hired servants, and went after him." While on a later occasion, Peter could confidently express their devotion to the Master, by saying in the name of them all: "Behold, we have forsaken all, and followed thee..." (Matt. 19:27, Mark 10:28, Luke 18:28). In yet another place, the meaning of this condition is explained as follows: "Another of his disciples said unto him, Lord, suffer me first to go and bury my father. But Jesus said unto him, Follow me, and let the dead bury their dead" (Matt. 8:21, 22). Here is, indeed, a stringent case of apparently conflicting calls; and it was doubtless in order to enforce His claim to the first place in the affection and obedience of His disciples, and the superior position, which the kingdom of God must occupy over all other relations of life in their esteem, that He here bade His disciple forego the earthly, that he might fulfill the heavenly duty.

Above all other reasonings, this should be born in mind, that in giving such a command as this to His disciples, He is but asking us to follow His own example. Of Himself it is true, that He left His Father's home and glory; of the Father it is true that He gave and delivered up His Son; and this in order to bring blessing to us. Then it ought to be to us not a strange, but a most natural call, that we should follow in His steps, and do for His sake and service what He did first for our salvation. "We love him, because he first loved us." Example as well as precept, reasons as well as command, consequences of blessing as well as conditions of consecration, He has given to us. It must be ours to follow the example and fulfill the precept, to accept the reasons and obey the command, to aim at the blessing and welcome the conditions; that He may have to the full what He gave His life to win: souls saved, hearts loyal, lives fruitful to the glory of the Father.

Each separate experience of individual disciples will surely find this condition of consecration working out in different ways. No one experience can be a perfect model for others. We differ one from another as the leaves of the forest, as the members of the body, as the stones of the temple, as the children in a family. But one fast extending branch of the church's service to Christ is today bringing into special prominence the practical application of this condition of consecration: "He that loveth father or mother more than me is not worthy of me: and he that loveth son or daughter more than me is not worthy of me." That service is the work of missions amongst the Jewish, the Mohammedan and the heathen races of the world. Practically speaking, it is true of every missionary, that he has made his choice between the Lord's call and nature's call of affection: he leaves his father and mother, that he may follow Christ. Oftentimes, he has to leave his wife for months and even years together. Generally, he has to part with sons and daughters for the work's sake. Now and again, it happens that even the life itself is given up for the Master. In almost every case of the foreign missionaries of the churches of Christ, the words of the Lord as to consecration and discipleship have been experimentally accepted: "If any man come to me, and hate not his father, and mother, and wife, and children, and brethren, and sisters, yea, and his own life also, he cannot be my disciple."

But the harvest is plenty, while the laborers are few. Even today, after 100 years of revived missionary interest and zeal, there are more Christian workers amid the five millions of London, than amid the one thousand millions of heathen and Mohammedan peoples. That means that 200 times as much attention is given to London alone, as to the crying needs of all the Christless world. And the churches of Christ are awakening to the fact that this cannot be the right issue of the Lord's command that all the world, all nations, every creature, and the uttermost part of the earth should hear His gospel and know His name. The call to consecration is a preliminary step to the evangelization of the world; and that call brings all who hear it face to face with this condition — that the Lord must have the first place in the heart's affections, the first claim upon the heart's obedience. A new factor is thus applied to the decisions of life in Christian families; and in two directions difficulties arise, corresponding to the two sections of the text in Matthew 10:37.

First, there is the case of son or daughter, who has hearkened to the call of God, and desires to go forth as a missionary, but is hindered by the refusal of the father's or mother's consent. Perhaps the case is less frequent with a son, who, in most cases, must after all make his own choice as to the life's calling, than with a daughter, whose home is with her parents. What does the text mean in her case? Is she so to apply it, that in spite of father or mother's refusal, she is to go out to the field? I think not: and that for two reasons. It is God's rule for the New Testament saints, as for the Old: "Honour thy father and mother..." (Eph. 6:2); and the first and principal way in which honor is rendered is that of obedience to commands and wishes. Wherever, therefore, a daughter is willing and ready to follow the missionary call, when the Holy Spirit has given it (Acts 13:2), and is prepared to forsake father and mother in so doing; there she has already put herself in obedience to the text, and is loving the Lord more than father or mother. But the heart being thus put right, and the natural love to parents being in subordinance to the love to God, it does not follow that the parents' command is to be disobeyed. If they should absolutely forbid the step, it would seem that obedience to the fifth command means that the daughter must not go counter to their will.

The second reason, which should guide a daughter in this case, arises from another consideration. Such a one can only go out to the foreign field in the right spirit, if she is expecting God to work with and through her; so that in answer to her prayers, and through her message, hard and dark hearts shall be turned to God and enlightened by the gospel. But with such an expectation of God's working abroad, surely it is a small thing to expect also His working at home, where already His Word is known and His name honored. If God means such a servant of His to prevail in prayer for heathen souls, it would seem the very simplest proof of His purpose, to let her prevail first at home, and by God's working to win the parents' consent.

The second clause of the text refers to father or mother, professing to be Christians, who are holding back son or daughter from the evident call of God. This is no case where one daughter alone is left, and the infirmities of a parent need and have a right to her attention and care. In all such cases, a "right judgment in all things" will surely make it plain, that no call of God is then summoning that daughter to the foreign field. But where no such claim or need exists, and yet the consent is refused, this text applies sharply. They want their children's companionship and loving attentions at home; they choose to keep them for their own enjoyment when God's call has plainly come; they decline to yield them up for the service of God; in a word, they "love son or daughter more than me." Where such a case exists, there needs to be an awakening to the infinitely solemn results of such a refusal. Where it is maintained, consecration does not exist, the heart's first affection is not given to God, the parent "cannot be Christ's disciple," and "is not worthy of Him."

Let the question be honestly faced in every family where it arises; let the oft-repeated profession, "Here we offer and present unto Thee ourselves," become at last an action: "Now therefore perform the doing of it …" (2 Cor. 8:11). Let the love of Christ constrain, and His reward attract you: you shall be worthy of Him, confessed by Him, a true disciple to Him, and a servant who brings glory to his Master.

In summarizing this chapter, we notice:
1. that the consecration of the priests in the Old Testament had a symbol of the heart's affections being given to God;
2. that the phrase of "hating father and mother" is explained by not "loving father or mother more than" Christ;
3. that the Lord's demand here, as the first condition of consecration, is that the first place in the heart's affections be given to Him;
4. that this implies that His love wants our love in return;
5. that the Old Testament enjoined, and the conduct of the apostles illustrated this condition;
6. that every missionary is an example of its fulfilment; and
7. that the calls of the mission fields of the world are the strongest test of our obedience to this condition.

Chapter 7
The Denial of Self

"…let him deny himself…"
(Matthew 16:24)

THE second particular of the conditions for consecration is thus stated by our Lord in the Gospel according to Matthew, and is given in identical words by Mark and Luke: "…If any *man* will come after me, let him deny himself…" (Matt. 16:24, Mark 13:34, Luke 9:23). And in order to show how universally applicable this condition is, we are told that it was addressed to the general audience of the people as well as to His disciples; forming thus a kind of elementary rule, to which all alike must submit, who wish to follow and come after Christ.

The exact meaning of the phrase "deny himself" will be discovered most simply by a comparison with the other passages in the New Testament where it occurs. Such a comparison is always helpful to a clear understanding of the Word of God, and a right explanation of it; for it is only by "comparing spiritual things with spiritual" that we are able to "…speak, not in the words which man's wisdom teacheth, but which the Holy Ghost teacheth…" (1 Cor. 2:13). But in the case of the particular phrase before us, such a comparison and search is specially necessary, because there is a widely accepted — indeed almost universal — use of the words, by which the real meaning is obscured if not destroyed; so that honest souls desiring to understand and obey the condition, are hindered and turned away from their purpose. In examining what is the regular scriptural usage and meaning of the phrase, we shall best expose and confute the misuse of it.

The first occurrence of the word "deny," with a person as the object of the denial, is found in Matthew 10:33: "But whosoever shall deny me before men, him will I also deny before My Father which is in heaven." The sense intended here is obvious, from the contrast afforded by the preceding verse:

Personal Consecration

"Whosoever therefore shall confess me before men, him will I confess also before My Father which is in heaven." Also the verses leading up to the text before us, describing the dangers and persecutions to which disciples of Christ will be liable, indicate that it is a question of confessing or denying Christ, when personal suffering or personal ease will be the result. In a similar connection, Paul writes in 2 Timothy 2:12: "If we suffer, we shall also reign with *him*; if we deny *him*, he also will deny us: ..." The underlying motive, which might lead a professed follower of Christ so to deny Him, is indicated probably by the sentence which follows the conditions we are considering, in the record of Mark (8:38) and Luke (9:26): "Whosoever therefore shall be ashamed of me and of my words in this adulterous and sinful generation; of him also shall the Son of man be ashamed, when he cometh in the glory of his Father with the holy angels." As an illustration of this being ashamed of Christ, of the failure to confess Him from the fear of consequent suffering, and thus of deliberate denial of Him, we turn to the story of the fall of Peter, where again the same word of "denying" is employed. Not only the fact, but the very manner and words of the denial are given to us, so that there can be no doubt as to the exact meaning intended. Thrice was he accused of being a companion of Jesus, and his denial was given in the words: "... I know not what thou sayest; ... I do not know the man; ... I know not the man" (Matt. 26:70, 72, 74). No clearer, or stronger, or simpler description can be desired of what is meant by "denying some one," than that it consists of saying and professing "I do not know the man," in answer to the challenge of your connection with him.

Another and slightly differing sense is developed when we read the accusation by which conviction of sin was brought home to the men of Jerusalem, in Acts 3:13, 14: "... Jesus, whom ye delivered up, and denied him in the presence of Pilate, when he was determined to let *him* go. But ye denied the Holy One and the Just, and desired a murderer to be granted unto you ..." The reference is not here to a question of personal acquaintance and relationship with Him, such as Peter denied in saying "I do not know the man," but to the acceptance or rejection of His claim to be the Messiah and King of Israel. These men who denied Him knew Him very well; they had seen and heard Him for a full three years; they had witnessed

His works by which the claim to Messiahship was established; and then at the real crisis of His life, when the final decision had to be made, whether they would own and accept Him as Messiah and King, they refused, they denied Him these titles, they rejected His claims, they disowned His rule. The actual words in which they thus denied Him are given to us: "Not this man, but Barabbas ... he ought to die, because he made himself the Son of God ... Away with *him* ... We have no king but Caesar" (John 18:40; 19:7, 15). Another illustration of the same use of the word is found in the speech of Stephen, when describing Israel's treatment of Moses. "He supposed his brethren would have understood how that God by his hand would deliver them: but they understood not ... He that did his neighbour wrong thrust him away, saying, Who made thee a ruler and a judge over us? ... This Moses, whom they refused, saying, Who made thee a ruler and a judge? the same did God send *to be* a ruler and deliverer ..." (Acts 7:25, 27, 35). The parallel between Moses and Jesus the Prophet, like unto Moses, is very exact. Each comes to his own people, with a claim and a title given him by God. Each puts forward that claim and offers its blessing to the people. Each is denied by Israel; that is, Israel refuses to accept the title and yield to its authority; they knew the man, but denied him in his character of the sent one of God.

Yet a third, and again somewhat different sense, is attached to the denying of Christ, as it is used by four of the Apostles in their writings. Paul writes of certain "unruly and vain talkers and deceivers," who "profess that they know God; but in works they deny *him*, being abominable and disobedient, and unto every good work reprobate" (Titus 1:16). Peter warns the church against "... false teachers among you, who privily shall bring in damnable heresies, even denying the Lord that bought them ..." (2 Pet. 2:1). John writes: "Who is a liar but he that denieth that Jesus is the Christ? He is antichrist, that denieth the Father and the Son. Whosoever denieth the Son, the same hath not the Father: ..." (1 John 2:22, 23). Jude describes how "... certain men crept in unawares ... ungodly men, turning the grace of our God into lasciviousness, and denying the only Lord God, and our Lord Jesus Christ" (Jude 1:4). In each of these cases — or at least in the first two and the last — denying is evidently employed in the sense of doing and teaching things contrary to the doctrine of Christ.

To profess His service is equivalent to saying that you are bound to obey Him, and are actually obeying Him now. If therefore there is an evident contradiction between such a profession and the conduct joined to it, there results in this sense a denial of Christ. The obedience due to Him is not rendered, and so His authority is denied, His name and place as Ruler are rejected. Paul suggests a possible case, in order to warn against it, where a man professing to be a Christian fails to provide for the needs of his own household and kindred. Such a case is so flagrantly contrary to the doctrine of the gospel, and so opposed to the whole principle of Christianity, that Paul says of such an one: "... he hath denied the faith, and is worse than an infidel" (1 Tim. 5:8).

With this threefold sense and meaning before us, in explanation of the way in which a person is said to deny another, we are ready to find a full and satisfactory solution of the phrase, "Let him deny himself." Everything which was done in these preceding cases towards Christ, a follower of Christ is required now to do towards himself. As the actual manner in which the word is used has been examined and described in these other passages, so we must in honesty apply it in the command of Christ to His followers, "Let him deny himself." And in so doing, it appears before us as a command of far more extended application than its common use would lead us to suppose. Since denying Christ means the opposite of confessing Him, when suffering attaches to confession and escape from suffering is the fruit of denial; so must denying self mean, that whenever personal comfort, ease or advantage, conflict with the following of Christ, such personal profit must be sacrificed; and so self is denied. Again, since denying Christ means the rejection of His claim as God's Ruler and King over men's lives; so must denying self mean, that a man rejects all claim to rule and govern his own life, and yields it in absolute subjection to the rule of Christ; and thus he denies himself. Once more, since denying Christ means the refusal to render Him the obedience He demands, and the denial of His authority over the conduct; so must denying self mean that the will of oneself shall no longer be obeyed, and the choice and decision of oneself no longer be recognized as the supreme authority and final umpire in the conduct of life; and thus self is denied. In fact, it comes to this in the end, "No man can serve two masters;" and the choice for life's service lies between Christ and self. When Christ is accepted and submitted to, obeyed and followed, as Master in the whole life, there self is denied and Christ confessed. But where self is the final authority; where the will, the pleasure, the choice and the decision of self is chosen in opposition and in preference to those of Christ, there Christ is denied and self is confessed as Lord. It is written that "by faith Moses, when he was come to years, he refused to be called the son of Pharaoh's daughter" (Heb. 11:24). In so doing, he gave a most practical illustration of the meaning of denying self. Everything of ease and comfort and advantage for himself depended upon his denying his Hebrew origin and the God of the Hebrews as his God. All loss of personal prosperity, of position and prospects in the Egyptian empire, was bound up with confessing the call of God, and denying himself. He chose the latter alternative: in "refusing to be called the son of Pharaoh's daughter," he denied himself, and confessed God as his Lord and Master. The life of service and of blessing followed upon that one decision.

Now there exists and prevails a very widespread and most general use of the phrase "denying self" or "self-denial," accepted almost everywhere both in the language of the churches and in the common parlance of the world, which stands in startling contrast to the meanings just deduced from the Scriptures. The true scriptural meaning is therein so toned down and attenuated, so diluted and curtailed, that in practice and conduct it totally evades the real point of the command: "Let him deny himself." In this common misuse of the word it is taken for granted, that "to deny something to oneself" is the same thing as self-denial or "denying self." Yet the difference between the two is infinite, the contrast is as wide as it can be. A man may "deny things to himself" all his life through, and yet may never once have even approached the idea, which Christ conveyed by saying "deny himself." A single illustration may serve to show how wide is the distinction between these two phrases and their meaning. Suppose that a young Jew asks his father to give him a gold watch, and his father replies,

Personal Consecration

"No, I must deny you that watch until you are older." Suppose again that that young Jew becomes a Christian, and, as has often happened, his father casts him out of house and home. If that son should come to his father and say, "Father, will you not let your son return to you?" the father answers, "I deny you; you are no son of mine; my son is dead; you are nothing to me." Now look at the contrast. In the former case, the father "denies something to his son"; but it makes very little difference to either of them, and they remain on the same terms as before. But in the latter case, the father "denies his son"; and thenceforth, they are severed as though they were utter strangers to one another, or even worse, as though they were enemies.

Let us take a few ordinary illustrations from everyday life to see how a man may deny things to himself without the least thought of denying himself. A man goes into training for a boat race, and immediately he denies to himself the use of stimulants, tobacco and other luxuries, which he generally enjoys. But he does it simply to please himself, and in the hope of winning the race. He counts the prize of the race worth the loss of the luxuries; and self is pleased and obeyed, but not denied, by the training. Or look at the student aiming at the attainment of high honors in an examination. He denies to himself much of amusement, recreations, time for ease and rest, in order that he may devote himself exclusively to his studies. The keen delight of reaching the highest success in the examination more than counter balances the years of voluntary hardship which preceded. He has pleased himself to the full, as the result of denying certain pleasures to himself. A boy who sets himself to save up his money in order to buy a watch; a musician who spends years in practice in order to attain high proficiency; a candidate for Parliament, who foregoes business profits, leisure time and personal ease, that he may canvas his constituents and gain his desired honor: all these and a thousand other cases exist around us, where people "deny themselves something," but never "deny themselves" in the scriptural sense.

This mistaken usage of the idea of denying self becomes most harmful when it prevails in religious thought and action. People suppose that, because they occasionally deny things to themselves, they are, therefore, in some sense obeying the Master's command: "Let him deny himself." To take the most common instance, very many religiously-minded people suppose that they are practicing self-denial as our Lord enjoined it, when during the forty days of Lent they abstain from some luxuries, amusements or indulgences to which they are at other times accustomed; and which they purpose resuming again when Lent is over. Such a course of action may very possibly be good for them, mentally, physically or spiritually; but it ought to be understood, that that is not what the Scripture means by self-denial. This process of denying themselves something for a time results in a saving of money; and what then is generally done with the money so saved? Perhaps the comic paper touched a wider range of cases than it thought, when it represented a young lady as saying: "After all, Lent is not such a bad thing. The money I saved by not buying sweets during Lent has paid for a new bonnet." Is there anything of confessing Christ, owning His authority, or obeying His commands, in this kind of falsely called self-denial? Self is thereby not denied at all, but simply profits in one direction by curtailing its expenditure in another. Self-denial does not consist in saying "No" to something you like, but in saying "No" to yourself.

Listen to the following case, as an illustration of the contrast between true and fictitious self-denial. Two men were conversing about the observance of Lent. The one says, that during Lent, he abstains from smoking; the other replies, that having found smoking a hindrance to his service of God, he abstains from it entirely. The former goes on to say, that during Lent he ceases going to theatres: the other answers, that he has come to the conclusion that the concomitants and moral atmosphere of theatres are not after the mind of Christ, and so he never goes to theatres. The first speaker adds, that during Lent, he does not dance; the latter states, that he has found the ballroom to be a place where he cannot consistently be a witness for Christ, and so he has ceased going to balls altogether. Now in the case of these two men, the ruling element is a different one; and it is the ruling element which decides the question of self-denial in the scriptural sense. The former man thought, no doubt, that it would be good for him to abstain from these things for the season of Lent, and he did so. But there could be no question of divine authority being substituted for his own choice in the matter. For if divine authority had ruled for him, that he must forsake these things, he could not have returned to them on Easter Monday, as he fully intended to do. But in the other case, the abstaining from these things depended on the fact, that he sought to be ruled by God in them. And without necessarily saying that God's guidance for him was the same He gives to all men, at least this is certain: he did not seek to rule and govern his own life, but sought to have it ruled by God. As he yielded obedience to what his own conscience conceived to be God's will, he practised in the truest sense the rule, "Let him deny himself."

One other consideration remains, by which the meaning of self-denial, which we have deduced from Scripture, is yet more strikingly enforced. The condition of self-denial, which we are considering as an essential part of consecration, is introduced by the sentence, "If any man will come after me." That, in itself, implies that the pathway along which Christ has gone before is one in which He has fulfilled the conditions which He is now putting upon His followers. It was as much as to say, "If any man will come after me, he must do what I have done." So then we may look at the example of Christ in order to discover what denying self means. And that example shows, as no other can do, how absolutely self-denial means the substitution of the divine will for the will of self in all the motives and conduct of life. When describing to the Jews what the hidden motives of His conduct and actions were, He made these remarkable statements: "... Verily, verily I say unto you, The Son can do nothing of himself, but what he seeth the Father do: for what things soever he doeth, these also doeth the Son likewise" (John 5:19). "I can of mine own self do nothing: as I hear, I judge: and my judgment is just; because I seek not mine own will, but the will of the Father which hath sent me" (John 5:30). "... as my Father hath taught Me, I speak these things" (John 8:28). "...I do always those things that please him" (John 8:29). "For I have not spoken of myself; but the Father which sent me, he gave me a commandment, what I should say, and what I should speak" (John 12:49). In these passages, we have the declaration that all the Saviour's actions, judgments, aims and words, were not His own, but His Father's. So completely had He yielded His own will, and accepted the Father's will and authority, that each single act, choice, decision and word was taken from the Father. Can any picture more fully show what He meant, when He joined "coming after me" with "denying self"?

The Apostles did and taught the same thing. "We then that are strong ought … not to please ourselves" (Rom. 15:1). "… they which live should not henceforth live unto themselves, but unto him which died for them, and rose again" (2 Cor. 5:15). "That he no longer should live the rest of *his* time in the flesh to the lusts of men, but to the will of God" (1 Pet. 4:2). "… we keep His commandments, and do those things that are pleasing in his sight" (1 John 3:22). In these and many other places, the great principle of true self-denial is enforced, that God's will and God's pleasure are to rule and decide the whole life of the disciple of Christ. In every possible divergence between your will and God's, self-denial consists in saying "No" to yourself, and "Yes, Lord" to God; and nothing less than that fulfills the call, "Let him deny himself."

In seeking how we may obediently fulfill this condition, it is of importance to notice that in the words, "Let him deny himself," the aorist tense of the verb is employed; by which is indicated a definite action, done once for all. So then here is a call to a life's decision, by which the conduct is henceforth to be ruled. Once and for all, from the moment that discipleship is entered upon and consecration becomes a reality, self is to be dethroned and Christ enthroned, as Ruler and Decider in all life's business and conduct. A position is to be assumed, and a relationship to Christ entered upon, by which the whole life is henceforth affected: no other rule but His, no other Lordship but Christ's, may be known: "… *other* lords beside thee have had dominion over us: *but* by thee only will we make mention of thy name" (Isa. 26:13).

To sum up the question of self-denial, it has been found:
    1. that denial has the threefold sense of the refusal to acknowledge acquaintance or relationship, the rejection of the claim of authority, the repudiation of obedience to commands;
    2. that self-denial therefore means the rejection of interference,

authority, or rule by man's self, and the substitution of Christ in the life;

3. that it is a complete misuse of the phrase, to confound the denying of something to oneself with the denying of self;

4. that many deny things to themselves, who never deny self;

5. that only there does self denial exist, where Christ takes the place of self for all life's decisions;

6. that the example of Christ is a perfect illustration of this true self-denial; and

7. that it implies a definite act and decision, as introductory to a life of consecration and discipleship.

Chapter 8
Bearing the Cross

"… let him … take up his cross, and follow Me."
(Matthew 16:24)

O F all the conditions for consecration which our Lord has named, none
has more emphasis laid upon it than the third in our order of study:
"If any *man* will come after me, let him … take up his cross, and follow
me" (Matt. 16:24). It is named on each of the three occasions when the
terms of discipleship are declared, and is further enforced on a separate
occasion for a single inquirer. Moreover, there is a certain variety in the
language employed in these various passages, which serves to develop with
remarkable fullness the exact meaning intended.

When speaking to the twelve apostles before their first mission journey,
the Lord says: "He that taketh not his cross and followeth after me, is not
worthy of me" (Matt. 10:38); and the word "take," means a personal receiving or accepting, the taking of a thing that is offered. This is the meaning
in John 1:12, "received him;" Matthew 26:26, "Take, eat;" and Revelation
11:17, "thou hast taken to thee." In the report given by the three evangelists
of the qualifications for discipleship, it reads: "Let him take up his cross,
and follow me," with the addition of the word "daily" by Luke (Matt. 16:24;
Mark 8:34; Luke 9:23). Here, the words "take up" have the meaning of
raising and lifting up something that lies on the ground in order to carry
it. Thus, it occurs in Matthew 9:6, " take up thy bed;" 14:12, "took up the
body;" 15:37, "took up of the broken *meat.*" In the address to the great
multitudes after the parable of the great supper, we read: "Whosoever doth
not bear his cross, and come after me, cannot be my disciple" (Luke 14:27).
The word "bear" means the carrying of something already lifted up: as in
Luke 7:14, "they that bare *him;*" 10:4, "Carry neither purse, nor scrip;"
22:10, "bearing a pitcher of water." In the further case of the rich young

man, our Lord said: "…come, take up the cross, and follow me" (Mark 10:21); using the same word as in Mark 8:34 above.

Moreover, we observe not only a significant variety in the verbs employed, but also a noteworthy distinction in the tenses of these verbs. Twice, the present tense is employed, by which a continuous course of action is indicated (Matt. 10:38; Luke 14:27); and in the other four passages, we have the aorist tense, by which a single act — definite and complete — is expressed. Before passing on to a more detailed study of the phrase, and a search into its exact meaning, two interesting points are already established by this preliminary examination of the language employed, which have a close bearing upon a disputed point.

Controversy has often arisen upon the question, whether consecration is in any sense a definite and decisive act, possibly referable to a given time, or must be considered as a continuous course of conduct, spread over a long period. The verbs and their tenses noticed in the passages above, suffice to give an answer to this question. There is an aspect of this condition, enforced by the words "take up," and the aorist tense of completed action in which it is used, which compels us to the conclusion, that there is something isolated and limited to a given time in the thought of consecration. Something lies before a soul, which it is required definitely to take up, in order that it may, henceforth, be carried. There then is the initial act, the conscious and deliberate step taken once for all. But three other indications are to be observed, by which it is equally certain, that the act of consecration thus done must be followed by a continuous line of conduct. There is the twofold present tense of the verbs "take" and "bear," by which perpetual action is expressed; as we might accurately render it: "Whosoever doth not bear his cross, he cannot be my disciple." There is the significant addition of the word "daily," even after the aorist tense of "take up" in Luke 9:23; so that the definite action once done, must have a constant repetition, as each day comes round. There is also the appended sentence, "come after me…and follow me," which is attached to each occurrence of the cross-bearing; and which, by the very sense of the word, must mean a perpetual walk and line of conduct. Here, therefore, as in so many other lessons of the divine life, a decisive step is demanded from the soul, as the response to a positive command; and then a life-long condition is intended to follow that first step, as the proof and evidence of the change which it introduced.

Turning now to the inquiry, as to the exact sense attached to the phrase "bearing the cross," we need to transport ourselves in thought to the time at which it was used by our Lord. The natural way in which the phrase is employed and repeated in the Gospels, without any particular explanation of it, suggests at once that it was an idea commonly understood by everybody, a simile that explained itself. The story of the crucifixion of our Lord Himself conveys the simplest solution of the question. "Then delivered he him therefore unto them to be crucified. And they took Jesus, and led *him* away. And he bearing his cross went forth ..." (John 19:16, 17). As that event took place, any stranger in the streets of Jerusalem, seeing Jesus bearing His cross, and questioned by us as to the meaning of the sight, would have said: "He is a criminal, condemned to death after his trial, and now on his way to execution." The fact that crucifixion was a common method of Roman capital punishment, and that the condemned culprit was made to carry his own cross, suffices to explain the simile to us. It is as though anyone in London during the last century had said of a passing procession: "They are on their way to Tyburn; they are riding in the hangman's cart." To see such a sight was to recognize a criminal: convicted, condemned and on his way to execution. When, therefore, our Lord speaks of His disciples as called to "bear their cross," He represents them as receiving from the world the character and treatment of a criminal: rejected, condemned, cast out and reviled.

Now this is exactly what our Lord had foretold, as the treatment they would meet with from a Christ-rejecting world. "Blessed are ye, when *men* shall revile you, and persecute *you*, and shall say all manner of evil against you falsely, for my sake ... Ye shall be hated of all *men* for my name's sake ... Then shall they deliver you up to be afflicted, and shall kill you: and ye shall be hated of all nations for my name's sake ... Blessed are ye, when men shall hate you, and when they shall separate you *from their company*, and shall reproach *you*, and cast out your name as evil, for the Son of man's sake … They shall put you out of the synagogues: yea, the time cometh, that whosoever killeth you will think that he doeth God service" (Matt. 5:11; 10:22; 24:9; Luke 6:22; John 16:2). All these methods of treatment by the world are just what they give to criminals and outcasts: and this is the meaning of "bearing the cross." So again, in the experience of Paul, we find him undergoing these very things, meeting just these trials, and called by such titles of reproach, as illustrate most clearly this meaning of the phrase we are examining. "… they went about to slay him … who persuaded the people, and, having stoned Paul, drew *him* out of the city, supposing he had been dead … the magistrates rent off their clothes, and commanded to beat *them*. And when they had laid many stripes upon them, they cast *them* into prison, charging the jailer to keep them safely: … they went about to kill him … *then* lifted up their voices and said, Away with such a *fellow* from the earth: for it is not fit that he should live … we will eat nothing until we have slain Paul … and we, or ever he come near, are ready to kill him … the Jews caught me in the temple, and went about to kill *me*" (Acts 9:29; 14:19; 16:22, 23; 21:31; 22:22; 23:14, 15; 26:21). Such is the historical record of the manner in which he was treated by even the religious world of his day; whilst extracts from his own letters fill in with abundance of detail the way in which he shared the "bearing of the cross."

In another passage, the phrase is slightly varied, and thereby, a very clear light thrown upon its meaning, when we read in Hebrews 13:12, 13: "Wherefore Jesus also, that he might sanctify the people with his own blood, suffered without the gate. Let us go forth therefore unto him without the camp, bearing his reproach." The parallel is noteworthy, when it is told of Him, that "He went forth, bearing his cross;" and we are bidden to "go forth, bearing his reproach." It is an explanation of what "bearing the cross" means in practical experience, that it is equivalent to "bearing the reproach" of Christ. To be a cross-bearing criminal is to be reproached by the world, as a wretch unfit to live; and to be a cross-bearing Christian is to meet with the reproach, which the world put upon Christ, when they hated Him without a cause, they all condemned Him to be guilty of death, and they cried out, "Away with *Him*, away with *Him*" (cf. John 15:25; Mark 14:64 ; John 19:15). Practically, we may sum up all that is meant by bearing the cross, as bearing and sharing the reproach of Christ, which He received at the hands of men.

In one of the Messianic psalms, which is applied to Christ not less than six times in the New Testament, and refers particularly to His crucifixion, there is frequent reference to His "reproach," and a very full description of what it meant and how it was brought upon Him. As we read the verses, there appear not less than six different elements in this reproach, all of which have their application to those disciples, who "go forth, bearing his reproach." The psalm in question, the sixty-ninth, gives first the three causes for which He was reproached. In verse 7, it is "... for thy sake I have borne reproach;" as in the New Testament it is "for my name's sake, for the son of man's sake," that reproach falls upon His disciples. In verse 9, it is "the zeal of thine house hath eaten me up; and the reproaches of them that reproached thee are fallen upon me;" and so in the case of Paul, his zeal for "... the house of God, which is the church of the living God ..." (1 Tim. 3:15), and for the spread of the gospel, whereby that house is built, brought on him the reproach of madness: "... thou art beside thyself ..." (Acts 26:24). The likeness between servant and Master, between the disciple and Lord is very marked, when we remember that the self-forgetting zeal of Christ led to the very same reproach: "when his friends heard *of it*, they went out to lay hold on him: for they said, He is beside himself" (Mark 3:21). In verses 10 – 11, it is said: "When I wept, *and chastened* my soul with fasting, that was to my reproach. I made sackcloth also my garment ..." So, in the prophets, we find the world's desire for pleasant and easy things; their hatred of the sorrow for sin; the sadness at suffering; and the grief at wrong-doing that mark the servants of God, leading them to say to the seers, "See not;" and to the prophets, "Prophesy not unto us right things, speak unto us smooth things, prophesy deceits ..." (Isa. 30:10). Again, our Lord contrasts the condition of disciples, poor in spirit, mourning for the evil around them, weeping over needy and lost souls, hungering for righteousness, with the world in its easy self-satisfaction, rich, comfortable, full, and laughing, faring sumptuously every day. (Matt. 5:44; Luke 6:20–25). We conclude that conduct which is maintained "for Christ's sake," zeal which is devoted to the good of the living church, sorrow and grief at prevailing evils, are the chief causes, which will bring the world's reproaches upon the Christian.

Then, in this sixty-ninth psalm, we notice also the forms which this reproach took, coming from three different quarters. In verse 8, "I am become a stranger unto my brethren, and an alien unto my mother's children." This was fulfilled in our Lord's case, when His brethren upbraided and believed not on Him (John 7:3 – 5, 10); and was forewarned as one of the results of following Him: "For I am come to set a man at variance against his father, and the daughter against her mother, and the daughter in law against her mother in law. And a man's foes *shall be* they of his own household" (Matt. 10:35, 36). In verse 9, "…the reproaches of them that reproached thee are fallen upon me," seems to refer to the sneering accusations of the Pharisees, that the poor and ignorant, the despised and degraded were those whom the Lord welcomed and taught (John 7:48, 49; Luke 15:1, 2). For it is stated that "Whoso mocketh the poor reproacheth his Maker …" (Prov. 17:5); and this verse of Psalm 69:9 is quoted in Romans 15:1, in immediate connection with the call " …to bear the infirmities of the weak, and not to please ourselves." In verses 11 and 12 of the Psalm, the result of bearing the marks of sorrow and grief was, "I became a proverb to them. They that sit in the gate speak against me; and I *was* the song of the drunkards." Three sets of people are here indicated, as joining in casting reproach upon the Saviour, when He became

> *"The by-word of the passing throng,*
> *The ruler's scoff, the drunkard's song."*

Alienation from one's own kinsfolk "for his sake"; sneers and reproaches from the prosperous world, for those who seek the outcast, the poor and needy, to bring them to Christ; mockery and ridicule from the careless worldling, the self-satisfied man of position, and the sin-bound slave of drink, against those who grieve over iniquity and sin, and lament the dominion of sin in men's souls: these are the forms of reproach which will come on those who are "bearing the cross."

An illustration of how these fell to the lot of one true disciple may be drawn from Paul's writings, where he says: "For I think that God has set forth us the apostles last, as it were appointed to death: for we are made a spectacle unto the world, and to angels, and to men. We *are* fools for Christ's sake…we *are* weak…we *are* despised…reviled…persecuted…defamed…we are made as the filth of the world, and are the offscouring of all things unto this day" (1 Cor. 4:9 – 13). The treatment of many a missionary among heathen and Mohammedans; the secret trials at home, in the workshop, among companions, of countless true disciples; the sneering nicknames given to faithful followers of Christ in our own day, are enough to tell us how real is the reproach for those who are "bearing the cross." This serves also to explain the meaning of the often misinterpreted phrase, "without the camp." A whole sect of modern Christians has assumed and taught, that "the camp" means any organized community or church of professed Christians; and then founds its appeal for all believers to join in their unorganized assemblies solely on this passage: "Let us go forth therefore unto him without the camp…" (Heb. 13:13). Practically, the question of the camp and its inhabitants depends upon the sentence following: "without the camp, bearing his reproach." The bearing of the reproach puts a soul outside, the refusal of it keeps him inside the camp. You may belong to any church in Christendom and yet be outside the camp, if you are bearing His reproach; and you may be outside all the churches and yet inside the camp if, in your life, you shirk and avoid the reproach and the cross of Christ.

It is by keeping to this strictly scriptural meaning of the phrase, "Let him take up his cross," that we discern the feeble unreality of the interpretation commonly attached to it. Everyone is familiar with the custom which prevails, whereby people call their poverty, or sickness, or uncongenial friends, or trying relatives, or even their bad temper, "their cross which they have to bear." Yet, tested by the language of Scripture, not one of these things is a cross or has anything to do with a cross. Sometimes the error is emphasized by an approved illustration: two sticks are placed crosswise, and taken to represent God's will and ours; so that whilst they are running in contrary directions, we are supposed to find God's will a cross to be borne; but when we yield to God's will, the cross disappears. The truth is found to be the exact opposite of this illustration. It is mainly by refusing God's will and way that the cross is escaped and avoided; and only when His will is fully accepted and obeyed does the cross-bearing really begin. The very terms of discipleship — "Let him take up his cross" — serve to show that whatever the cross is, it is something that can either be taken or left, chosen or declined. Now poverty and sickness and the lack of sympathy, and the existence of irritable relatives near us, none of these things are a matter of choice: where they exist they exist, and you cannot avoid them. So then these cannot be the cross. But what shall we say of an evil, hasty or bad temper? Can this be the cross which the Lord bids His disciples take up and bear? Not for a moment. A bad temper is not a cross, but a crime; and the sooner it is recognized as totally alien to the spirit of Christ, an evil to be confessed and to be delivered from, the better for the soul that is bound by it. Let there be no self-deception about these things: they are not the cross, they form no object of choice, they are not conditions of discipleship, they do not belong to the idea of the reproach of Christ.

But ere we close this chapter and branch of consecration truth, let it be a matter of personal consideration to us, that this cross-bearing is a matter for choice and decision, for definite and initial action, for continuous and permanent conduct, in the true disciple of Christ. A matter for choice, not in the sense that the Christian is at liberty to choose it or not, but as something upon which he is bound to exercise his choice and decide for Christ's service; just as each soul that hears the call, "How long hath ye between two opinions?" is bidden to decide for Christ's salvation. A matter for definite action following upon the choice, and actually taking up the offered cross in the service of Christ. A matter also for permanent effect on conduct, a daily fresh apprehension of the position once assumed, a taking up anew of the reproach of Christ as we go forth into the world for the round of the daily life. Paul writes in one place of "... that which cometh upon me daily, the care of all the churches" (2 Cor. 11:28). With him, doubtless every church he founded was home at once upon his heart, to care for it as long as he lived; yet also there was daily a fresh assumption of care for it, "Always in every prayer of mine for you all making request with joy ..." (Phil. 1:4). Thus, is the disciple who would be consecrated to Christ's service bidden to assume once for all, and to resume day by day, the cross and the reproach, and to bear it after Jesus.

In summary of this topic, we notice:

1. that the variety of words and tenses employed, serve to show that in consecration there is both a definite commencement and a continuous conduct demanded;

2. that "bearing the cross" meant originally to have the character of a condemned and rejected criminal in the eyes of the world;

3. that such treatment was foretold by our Lord, and endured by Himself and His apostles;

4. that another expression for the same thing is "bearing the reproach of Christ";

5. that this reproach follows wherever there is a life lived for Christ's sake, wherever a zeal for God's house and a heart-grief over evils within it, are ruling characteristics;

6. that it will often mean alienation from friends, and always ridicule, sneers, and hatred from the world that hated Christ;

7. that this reproach is the factor which gives fellowship with Christ "without the camp";

8. that to explain the cross by the ordinary trials of life or the faulty defects of character is a total misuse of the phrase; and

9. that it is a matter for personal choice, definite action, and continuous practice by every faithful disciple of Christ.

Chapter 9
Life Saved and Lost

"Whosoever will save his life shall lose it: and whosoever will lose his life for My sake shall find it."
(Matthew 16:25)

CLOSELY connected with the words about bearing the cross — and occurring also in each of the three descriptions of discipleship — is the next condition and step in consecration, given in these terms: "For whosoever will save his life shall lose it: and whosoever will lose his life for my sake shall find it" (Matt. 16:25). In the parallel passage of Mark 8:35, there is a slight addition: "for my sake and the gospel's;" and both there and in Luke 9:24, for "find it," the closing words are "save it." The same statement occurs in Matthew 10:39, and is abbreviated in Luke 14:26 into the short phrase: "hate ... yea, and his own life also." Besides these direct expressions of this further condition, it appears in two other places as a principle of application to every Christian life, and one that is illustrated in the life of the Master Himself. When warning the disciples of the return of the Son of Man, and likening that day to the time of Noah in the coming of the flood and the time of Lot in the overthrow of Sodom, our Lord points out the real condition of preparedness in these words: "Remember Lot's wife. Whosoever shall seek to save his life shall lose it; and whosoever shall lose his life shall preserve it" (Luke 17:32, 33). The other occasion is that of the Greeks at the last Passover in the Gospels coming to Philip, and saying, "Sir, we would see Jesus." Upon receiving this report, our Lord answered thus: "... The hour is come, that the Son of man should be glorified. Verily, verily, I say unto you, Except a corn of wheat fall into the ground and die, it abideth alone: but if it die, it bringeth forth much fruit. He that loveth his life shall lose it: and he that hateth his life in this world shall keep it unto life eternal" (John 12:23 – 25). The context seems to imply that our Lord here gives the condition, on which alone He could be known to seek souls throughout the world, and gather in the much fruit from other lands, to which His commands after resurrection chiefly refer. Only after "the sufferings of Christ" could there be "the glory that should follow" (1 Pet. 1:11); for the Master as for the servants the principle must hold, that only by losing the life can it be found, saved and kept in the truest sense.

The wide application of this principle may be seen by the varying circumstances under which it was applied. Spoken to the Twelve when commissioned for their first evangelistic journey, it defines the spirit in which this and all future service must be undertaken; without it, they would not be "worthy" messengers (Matt. 10:38, 39). Repeated to the disciples with the multitudes, it pressed home the real issues of profit and loss in the eternal glory, as decided by the attitude of the soul in this life (Matt. 16:25 – 27). Addressed to the great multitudes, it enforced the absorbing demands of true discipleship (Luke 14:26). Uttered in connection with the prophecy of the Second Advent, it revealed wherein the preparation for that coming actually consists. Given to the disciples in response to the appeal of the Greeks, it unfolds the method, in Master and servants alike, by which the gospel will be carried to the world's end. The frequency of repetition, the diversity of application, for this principle, is good reason for searching carefully into its exact meaning, and endeavoring to bring its full force to bear upon our lives today.

The only way in which something can be permanently found, gained or kept in the world to come, is by deliberately losing it in this world. Now this cannot possibly be the "soul," in the sense ordinarily implied by the word; for the Lord came to save men's souls, and could not in any way mean that they should be lost. But it can be, and no doubt it is what we understand by the "life," which if given up and lost to all sense of personal profit and gain for the sake of Christ and the gospel, will be found to have been wholly gained in the world to come. In this sense, verse 26 further expresses the same thought: that no amount of personal advantage now can make up for the loss of a wasted life hereafter. The use of the word "life" is, therefore, consistent throughout the two verses.

It is well once more to insist that discipleship is not the condition of salvation of the soul, but the consequence of it. In the matter of salvation, there is no question of reward gained or lost; it is a free gift imparted and received. Hence, these verses that deal with the gaining or missing of reward cannot refer directly to the salvation of the soul. But discipleship implies service, and to service, the gaining or losing of a reward is distinctly attached. The words about crowns, prizes, recompense, rewards, gain, and glory are ever in connection with service faithfully rendered; and the loss of these possible possessions follows upon failure of faithful service. Such then is the topic before us: not the saving or losing of the soul, but the life — reckoned as gained or lost — according as it is yielded up to the Master's service, or withheld from Him and kept for selfish ends. The world that knows not Christ is accustomed to use practically the same language. When it hears of some man of marked ability and power giving up his life for missionary work among the degraded and outcast of our own or heathen lands, it calls such a life thrown away, wasted, lost. It reckons that he has lost the chance of making a name, a fortune or a mark in history; and thinks him a fool for his pains. But the Lord bids us look the other side of the veil, and weigh things in the balances of the sanctuary. Then it appears that a life thus lost, as the world names it, is really saved, gained and kept; whilst the life spent for worldly advantage, earthly profit, and selfish ends counts but as pure loss, and is worth nothing in His sight.

Our Lord's use of the idea of losing and keeping the life, in John 12:24, 25, applies it to Himself and His own conduct, and once more makes Him the example for disciples to follow. We have already seen how all the other conditions of discipleship were fulfilled by Him, ere He laid them down as rules for His disciples. He left His Father's throne and presence, that He might come to earth for man's salvation; so He bids us not to love father or mother more than Him. He denied Himself with such absolute completeness, that His very judgments, words, actions and will were not His own but the Father's; and thus, He bids us to deny self and follow Him. He took up the cross, figuratively, as the reproach He bore for God and His house, and, literally, on the way to Calvary; and then bids us to take up the cross likewise. Now also, in urging upon disciples the call to lose their life here, that it may prove all gain up there, He shows that He has gone before along this path and done the same Himself which He bids us do. For Himself as for us, the principle is true—only through death comes full life, only through apparent loss comes real gain, only through suffering comes the glory to follow. "Verily, verily, I say unto you, except a corn of wheat fall into the ground and die, it abideth alone: but if it die, it bringeth forth much fruit." Here is the picture of His life laid down, given up, and lost, as the only way by which it could produce the much fruit of a world-wide church and an innumerable multitude of saved souls. "He that loveth his life shall lose it; and he that hateth his life in this world shall keep it unto life eternal." This is the principle upon which He acted Himself, and to which reference is frequently made elsewhere: "I am the good shepherd: the good shepherd giveth his life for the sheep ... I lay down my life for the sheep ... I lay it down of myself ... Greater love hath no man than this, that a man lay down his life for his friends ... he laid down his life for us ... the Son of man came ... to give his life a ransom for many ... " (John 10:11, 15, 18; 15:13; 1 John 3:16; Matt. 20:28).

This principle of our Lord's own action is from the context of John 12:25, evidently meant to be applied to His followers also; for the next verse goes on: "If any man serve me, let him follow me; and where I am, there shall also my servant be: if any man serve me, him will *my* Father honour." Thus also the verse 16 of 1 John 3 joins His example and our commanded practice together: "... he laid down his life for us: and we ought to lay down *our* lives for the brethren."

The example of the Saviour was accepted by the apostles as one to be followed in the most literal sense. A few quotations out of many will suffice to show how they acted upon this principle and fulfilled this condition of losing, hating, and giving up their lives for Christ's sake and the gospel's, that they might find and keep and save them in the world to come. To the Ephesian elders, Paul said, "...neither count I my life dear unto myself,so that I might finish my course with joy ..." and to the brethren at Cesarea: "... I am ready not to be bound only, but also to die at Jerusalem, for the name of the Lord Jesus" (Acts 20:24–25; 21:13). Of Priscilla and Aquila, he wrote as: "… my helpers in Christ Jesus: Who have for my life laid down their own necks…" thus, most practically, were they willing to "lay down their lives for the brethren" (Rom. 16:3, 4). Of Epaphroditus, again he says, "… for the work of Christ he was nigh unto death, not regarding his life, to supply your lack of service to me" (Phil. 2:30). And of the victorious saints, it is said in heaven, "… they loved not their lives unto the death" (Rev. 12:11).

Old Testament phraseology gives some further help in illustrating this condition of a life lost for Christ and the gospel's sake, when we read of three heroes under the old dispensation these words: "My father fought for you, and adventured his life far, and delivered you…"; "…I put my life in my hands, and passed over against the children of Ammon, and the LORD delivered them into my hand…"; "He did put his life in his hand, and slew the Philistine, and the LORD wrought a great salvation for all Israel…" (Judg. 9:17; 12:3; 1 Sam. 19:5). In each of these cases, the condition on which deliverance was wrought and effective service rendered, was that the warrior disregarded his own life and was willing to give it up; by so doing, he saved both his own life and that of countless oppressed brethren. And in each case, if the warrior had shrunk from the risk and the sacrifice, the service had not been rendered, the deliverance for Israel had not been wrought, aye, and perhaps the very life he was trying to keep from risk might have fallen forfeit to the enemy. The analogy with our Lord's New Testament teaching is very close and real; the heroes of faith in all ages must be distinguished by the same principles of action, however varied the scenes of their exploits and the circumstances by which their heroism is tested.

The condition for consecration and discipleship, which calls for a practical surrender of the whole life, and a willingness to let it be lost to all personal ends for Christ's sake, forms in fact the summary and climax of all that has gone before. It meets also the possible objection, which may so easily rise in the mind, when these conditions of discipleship are enforced, that really by this series of demands, the whole being is put under contribution and nothing is left unclaimed by Christ. If my heart's affections are asked for, my will and desires made subject, the Lord and His word become the consuming aim of existence. What is there left for myself to enjoy and possess? Practically nothing, for the whole life is included in these things, and must be given up if they are really done. But that is just what our Lord means that we should do: give up the whole life for Him, use and occupy it all as His, so that there is nothing left which is not at His disposal and under His control. Such a course of conduct, the world which knows not Christ, and the carnal portion of the church, which cares not to know Him fully, will always consider exaggerated beyond the bounds of reason, and really a waste of the life. So it is indeed, if we look no further than the "this world" of John 12:5: for it foregoes the only aims and attainments which the world thinks profitable, the pleasures and profit of time and sense and sight. But as soon as the "life eternal" comes in as a factor, and faith instead of sight brings in its reckoning, all things assume a different aspect. This life of ours is seen to have a twofold value: it may be so spent as to obtain all temporal success and profit, and to leave nothing over for the reckoning in the other world; or it may be expended solely with an eye to eternal gains, leaving this world out of account as not worth considering in comparison. The children of this world show something of this spirit in an elementary form when, in order to provide for the future comfort of wife and children, they curtail their own luxuries, and make provision for their possibly early death by life insurance or some other form of savings. The children of light should see further and carry out the same principle to its logical issue; so using this life on earth, that it may count as all profit in the life eternal; so welcoming its loss (as the world will count it) here, that it may be found, saved and kept, for the eternity there.

In the three parallel places of the Synoptic Gospels, this demand for a life yielded up to the Lord is followed immediately by a reference to the coming of the Son of Man in the glory of the Father, and to the rewarding of service which will then take place (Matt. 16:27; Mark 8:38; Luke 9:26). Only in view of that time can these conditions of consecration be seen in their real light: that the Lord is not herein laying down hard rules, to embitter the life and sap its enjoyment; but is teaching how it can be spent to the highest advantage, and how to fill it with the greatest fullness of heavenly joy. Let in the light of the Second Advent upon our lives, and we have the real test as to their profitable use. When that day comes, there will be some whom the Lord will confess before His Father and the assembled angels, and whom He will reward with incorruptible crowns and prizes of eternal glory; and there will be others of whom He will be ashamed in that glorious company, and who will be "ashamed before Him at His coming." This life and the way it is spent will decide the alternative of shame or glory then: consecrated lives of true discipleship will share an eternal weight of glory; but wasted lives of earthly self-seeking will be found then a cause of present shame and eternal loss.

The final reason upon which the Master grounds His demands for such consecration should not be left unnoticed. "For my sake," "for my sake, and the gospel's," He asks a yielded life. It gives us alike His own thought about it, and affords us the true answer, which we should give to a questioning world. The world understands the total absorption of a life spent in devotion to scientific researches, mechanical inventions, and classical studies; and it explains the loss in such a life of many other things usually desired, by the simple phrase: "He lives for science, for invention, for study." It should be our glory to show a nobler cause and a grander reason than any of these, to proclaim a far more enduring renown and a much higher object, when we say of our lives and of their consecration to God: "it is for Christ's sake and the gospel's." Paul thought all was well lost and nothing worth considering in comparison, if only he might "win Christ" in His fullness. If a noble aim honestly pursued means a noble life, there can be none more noble than a life spent "for Christ's sake."

In summarizing this chapter, we note:
1. that the subject concerns the method in which the life of the Christian is spent;
2. that the method in which it is spent on earth will decide the value to be attached to it in the glory;
3. that if kept and saved here for selfish or earthly ends, it will prove to have been lost for eternal value;
4. that by being yielded, given up, and lost to earthly aims and profits, it will prove to have been gained, saved, and kept eternally;

5. that our Lord's example, and that of apostolic men, explains the meaning, and the Old Testament illustrates it;

6. that it forms the climax of consecration, and is to be tested in view of the Second Advent; and

7. the powerful plea by which it is demanded, is "for Christ's sake and the gospel's."

Chapter 10
Counting the Cost

"Which of you, intending to build a tower, sitteth not down
first, and counteth the cost…?"
(Luke 14:28)

THE last chapter brought into prominence the idea of profit and loss,
the gaining of a reward or incurring of a fine, in relation to the life
spent here on earth. The last of the conditions of discipleship, which will
form the substance of the next chapter, is introduced by a remarkable
passage, occurring only in the Gospel according to Luke, and which lays
great stress upon this same question of profit and loss in the earthly life
of the Christian. The passage runs thus: "For which of you, intending to
build a tower, sitteth not down first, and counteth the cost, whether he have
sufficient to finish *it*? Lest haply after he hath laid the foundation, and is
not able to finish *it*, all that behold *it* begin to mock him, Saying, This man
began to build, and was not able to finish. Or what king, going to make war
against another king, sitteth not down first, and consulteth whether he be
able with ten thousand to meet him that cometh against him with twenty
thousand? Or else, while the other is yet a great way off, he sendeth an
ambassage, and desireth conditions of peace" (Luke 14:28 – 32).

A double parable is here given to those who would be disciples, employ-
ing two similes, which are elsewhere applied to Christians: that of a builder
and that of a soldier (see 1 Cor. 3:12; 2 Tim. 2:3). In each case, the simile is
adapted for one and the same purpose: to bring before the soul the immense
importance of counting the cost; thereby implying that the end in view
cannot be attained except at a certain cost, that the question of that cost
ought to be most thoroughly weighed, and that only after the most careful
consideration ought the final decision to be made. This necessity for deliberation applies equally to the conditions of discipleship already considered,
and to the final one which is to follow. The similes are connected with the

89

preceding conditions by the word "for," and with the succeeding condition by the word "so" (Luke 14:28, 33). All these steps and conditions, each in turn, and the whole subject of consecration, are thus shown to be matters which do not come about of themselves, without any deliberation, choice, decision or action of the soul. It seems as if this were a point that needed the solemn emphasis here given to it; for apparently, very many people, assured of their position as believers in Christ, and claiming their title as Christians, do not consider that they are called upon for any further decision about following Christ. They know that there was need for decision about repentance and faith, about conversion and coming to Christ; but as for any further steps to follow, they will develop of themselves, they will follow as a matter of course, they will gradually find their place in the life; there is no need to take any further trouble or thought about them. So men appear to reason.

The teaching of our Lord in the passage now before us is the very opposite of this. If we listen to it, we shall find that it is the strongest call to deliberation and decision upon this question of consecration, quite as emphatically as upon the question of conversion. These spiritual conditions and blessings do not come as a matter of course, they are not equally evident in all professedly Christian lives; and for this very reason, that this summons of the Master to make a matter of business calculation, and of conscious and definite decision about them, is too frequently and widely ignored. In this light, we will look at the twofold simile employed, and turn to personal use the demand therein conveyed to us, upon the subject of discipleship.

The parable of the builder is one that commends itself at once to the common sense of every hearer. In this, as in many other matters, the children of this world are wiser in their generation than the children of light. "For which of you, intending to build a tower, sitteth not down first, and counteth the cost, whether he have sufficient to finish it." A definite object is here depicted as occupying a human mind: he intends, he wishes, he wills, to build a tower. In order to carry it out effectively, and attain his wish, he is represented as doing three things. First, he sits down: he takes the attitude of quiet deliberation and of lengthened attention. This is not a matter to be decided by a passing impulse, on the spur of the moment, without time for thought. So he sits down. Next he "counteth the cost": he draws up his balance-sheet, estimates the expenditure, allows for possible additions, puts the outlay at the highest figure on the one side; and on the other, he places the amount at his disposal, the convenience with which he can produce the money, and possibly the extent to which he can safely afford to exceed his immediate reserve funds, and depend upon prospective income. Lastly, he comes to a decision "whether he have sufficient to finish it," before he begins the work at all. If he should fail to take these steps and carefully work through the course depicted, the alternative is vividly portrayed: he lays the foundation, the walls begin to rise, then progress is arrested, and every passer-by mocks the builder for his folly. This is no fancy picture. In our own country, frequent cases occur, where some half-finished tower or ruined pile is called somebody's "Folly," a warning and a memento of the Saviour's words.

The application of this to the soul of anyone who would be a disciple is evident at once; yet how often and how widely is it overlooked. It connects with discipleship and consecration the three steps just considered. It bids the Christian sit down first: here is a business transaction intended that calls for calm and deliberate treatment; much of infinite importance hangs in the balance. It bids him next to count the cost; to reckon and estimate how much he will have to spend and forego and surrender, if the work is to be completed; to calculate how long it will take him, and what demands it will make; to balance the gain he hopes to acquire with the loss he is likely to suffer. Then it bids him come to a decision, whether it is worthwhile, worth the cost, worth carrying through at any price; and upon that decision to act and live. The alternative is true in the soul as in the body: that if one starts on such a life of consecration, and then fails to go through with it, from lack of deliberation and calculation at the start, he becomes a subject for mockery by the world. A certain man made public confession of faith in a surrender to Christ; whereupon his worldly friends lamented together that they would lose the enjoyment of the worldly entertainments for which his house had been noted. Not long after, these entertainments were resumed, and the profession allowed to fade away; with the result that the very friends who had respected, though they lamented, his change, now mocked at it and said: "After all, it has not made much difference." The world which rejects the claims of Christ has often a keener apprehension of what those claims demand, than the Christian who is careless about obeying them. The world can respect, even if it hates, the thorough disciple; but it mocks, even while it welcomes, the half-hearted and backsliding professor of religion.

The second simile enforces in the main the same lesson, though under different circumstances and in view of an even more solemn alternative. The parable of the king, "going to make war against another king," presents the same three steps of deliberation as the parable of the builder. He sits down first; for a matter of serious import, calls for careful thought, affecting as it does himself, his throne, and his people. Next, "he consulteth whether he be able with ten thousand to meet him that cometh against him with twenty thousand." Here is need for more cautious calculation, for clear apprehension, and accurate knowledge, not only of his own forces and their value, but the comparative value and numbers of the opposing host. The ten thousand Greeks under Xenophon were worth ten times their number of undisciplined and effeminate Persians; but they could not have conquered even an equal ten thousand, such as Rome produced in her prime. Then comes the decision and the alternative: either the confidence of victory, and the bold incurring of every risk to gain it; or the prudent avoidance of danger before it comes too near, and a humble submission to the terms of peace.

Again, the parallel holds good for the Christian. He is to make it a matter of calm and business-like consideration, of thorough and deliberate calculation, and of a final and lasting decision. The actual force of the simile, as far as it touches the opposing king, is perhaps open to a double interpretation. It may indicate the forces arrayed against the Christian in his way to heaven, and the need to obtain divine power upon his own inadequate strength, if he is to meet them successfully. Then the decision would be like that of the man in "Pilgrim's Progress," who sees the staircase filled with armed men to resist any passage to the realm of glory above; but he counts the cost, girds on his armour, determines to win his way through, and bids the writer put down his name for the conflict. Such may be the Christian's decision, to face every obstacle boldly, and incur every loss, rather than miss the glory of the reward.

But the parable may have another meaning, akin to the warning of Christ in Matthew 5:25, 26 : "Agree with thine adversary quickly, whiles thou art in the way with him; lest at any time the adversary deliver thee to the judge, and the judge deliver thee to the officer, and thou be cast into prison. Verily I say unto thee, Thou shalt by no means come out thence, till thou hast paid the uttermost farthing." Here it would seem that God is the adversary of the unrepenting sinner, to whom the most urgent advice comes home to agree with God quickly, while life yet lasts. And it may be that the opposing king, with his overwhelming forces, represents God as He will meet the professed Christian at life's end. Such an aspect serves at least to give great force to the idea of the soul desiring "conditions of peace"; and indicates that it is the highest wisdom to find out now, upon what terms we may meet Him with joy and not fear, with boldness and not shame, when this life is ended and the other begins. Whilst some uncertainty exists, and rival commentators take opposite views upon this minor point of interpretation, there is no room for doubt or divergence upon the main point: that these two parables press home, with intense earnestness, the need for calm deliberation, careful calculation, and conclusive decision about the whole question, and the various conditions of discipleship and consecration.

But when this is in some measure attempted, when souls do at least partially weigh the question of profit and loss connected with whole-hearted service of Christ, there may still occur a mistake, which needs to be warned against and avoided. The matter is taken up thus: "If I determine to follow Christ wholly, I shall lose this line of business advantage, and forfeit that prospect of larger gains; I shall have to leave this form of recreation, forego that line of pleasures, and avoid these circles of friendship. I must give up this, let go that, and have done with the other thing. The loss is enormous; it is more than I am willing to endure; it is not fair to ask it of me." In this way, the eyes being fixed on the earthly loss, it bulks so largely that all else is put out of proportion, and the wrong decision is made. There is another, a wiser and a truer method of calculation.

Let the soul reckon and estimate, not what it will lose of earthly things if it follows Christ wholly, but what it will lose of heavenly things now, and in eternity, if it does not follow Christ fully. Put it in these terms: "What shall I miss of present peace, present blessing, present usefulness and service, present fruitfulness and glory to God; and what shall I lose of future reward and recompense, future glory and happiness, future praise of God, if I do not take up the terms of discipleship and consecrate my life to Him?" That was the way in which the heroes of Scripture made their estimate; and in the power of such a calculation the true decision was gained.

Look at some examples of such a counting of the cost. When our Lord was enforcing the need for leaving all to follow Him, and Peter had asked the reward for doing so, He answered: "... Verily I say unto you, There is no man that hath left house, or brethren, or sisters, or father, or mother, or wife, or children, or lands, for my sake, and the gospel's, But he shall receive an hundredfold now in this time, houses, and brethren, and sisters, and mothers, and children, and lands, with persecutions; and in the world to come eternal life" (Mark 10:29, 30). A proper counting of the cost will therefore put down the loss of ten thousand percent — for such is the value of "an hundredfold" — to everyone who refuses to leave aught that stands in the way of discipleship. Again, when Paul counted the cost, he reckoned "... that the sufferings of this present time *are* not worthy *to be compared* with the glory that shall be revealed in us" (Rom. 8:18); he declared that "... our light affliction, which is but for a moment, worketh for us a far more exceeding *and* eternal weight of glory" (2 Cor. 4:7); he counted the seven topics of human righteousness he possessed to be "... *but* loss for the excellency of the knowledge of Christ Jesus my Lord" (Phil. 3:8). Again, of Moses, we are told the double comparison he made, "Choosing rather to suffer affliction with the people of God, than to enjoy the pleasures of sin for a season; Esteeming the reproach of Christ greater riches than the treasures of Egypt: for he had respect unto the recompense of the reward" (Heb. 11:5, 26). Once more, in the second and third chapters of Revelation, there is put before us a sevenfold reward and glory to be gained, by those who consent to the sevenfold conditions of overcoming. Surely, here are found the materials for calculation, and a right estimate of profit and loss. Who can endure to lose such glories, both present and eternal, for the fleeting and illusive profit of a passing moment? Let us sit down, count the cost, and decide for God.

The principle of the true Christian life is given in the words, "We walk by faith, not by sight" (2 Cor. 5:7); and nowhere is the victory over sight more needed than when balancing the matters of profit and loss in the service of Christ. The rewards, the prizes, the recompense, the glory are invisible to the earthly sight; faith must apprehend them and bring them into account. But when faith thus acts, and when the soul sits down to put faith's estimate, founded on God's promises, upon the balance-sheet, then surely there can be no question as to the conclusion. It ought not to be hard or strange to anyone who, by trust in the Word of God, has found the beginning of the Christian life, to go on upon that word in proving the development and fullness of that life. The condition for such vision of faith, and such right and wise decision, is fulfilled, "While we look not at the things which are seen, but at the things which are not seen: for the things which are seen *are* temporal; but the things which are not seen *are* eternal" (2 Cor. 4:18).

In summary, we notice briefly:
    1. that the Lord enforces a lesson with a double parable, in connection with the conditions of discipleship;
    2. that the lesson enjoins deliberation, calculation and decision upon all would-be disciples;
    3. that the question of profit and loss depends upon the decision;
    4. that the loss to be considered is, not only earthly loss from following Christ, but earthly, heavenly and eternal loss from not following Christ;
    5. that the heroes of Scripture thus acted; and
    6. that by faith we can do the same.

Chapter 11
Forsaking All

"So likewise, whosoever he be of you that forsaketh not all that he hath, he cannot be My disciple."
(Luke 14:33)

THE last of the conditions of discipleship is now before us, connected with those that have already been considered by the solemn appeal to "count the cost." That appeal was joined to the preceding conditions by its introductory "for": "For which of you... sitteth not down first, and counteth the cost..."; and it is as closely applied to this last sentence by the "so likewise" of the text. The whole series of conditions, which are the real principles of personal consecration, has been working outwards from the heart, and with this last one has reached the furthest outer limit of the individual life. From the demand for the first place in the affections we passed, through the displacement of self from the position of ruler in the life, to the cross-bearing of the reproach of Christ at the hands of the world. Then the surrender of the life itself is asked, with the wise estimate of what it costs and what it gains by doing so; and now we have come to that which is quite on the outside of the man, not himself in any sense, but the possessions attached to him and the things he calls his own.

We noticed the same order of things in the offerings of the priest at his consecration: first, the fat, symbolizing the riches of the heart's affections; then the right shoulder, to indicate the powers of the body and the life; and last, the bread from the basket, as representing the man's goods and possessions, his "basket and store." It seems, therefore, to be an intentional and normal order of things, that in consecration and discipleship, as in every other aspect of the divine life in man, everything must begin from the center and work out to the circumference. The heart, the foundation, the root, the inner man, must first be set right with God; then through the mind renewed, the aims sanctified, the motives cleansed, the eye made single, we pass to the bodily powers yielded to God; and reach at last the goods and possessions to be consecrated and treated as His.

In Old Testament times, instructions were given in relation to the claims of God on a man's outward possessions with extreme minuteness. The tithe for the support of the Levites, the second tithe for use at the stated festivals, the regular order of first-fruits and offerings, and the surrender of all advantage from the fruits of Sabbatic year: these rules laid out with much exactness the demands of God for the consecration of Israel's possessions to Him. But in the New Testament, such particular injunctions have disappeared, as marking the infantile stage of the soul's growth; and in their place are given great principles, intended to be worked out with the intelligence of full-grown and mature souls. Such a principle, nay, rather the sum of such principles, is conveyed with a wide and grand comprehensiveness, when the Lord said: "So likewise, whosoever he be of you that forsaketh not all that he hath, he cannot be my disciple."

It is commonly said, in a kind of proverbial utterance, that the last part of a man to be converted is his pocket. It would be more scriptural to change the word "converted" — which implies God's action — into the word "consecrated" — which is God's demand for man's action. Then we shall see that normally and literally, the last part of man which he is called to consecrate, and the part which most conclusively proves his consecration, is his outward possessions, his purse and his property. Last, as it is in the divine order, it seems also to be very decidedly the last in human apprehension; for there is probably no aspect of the whole subject of consecration, in which the living church as a whole is more dull of apprehension, sluggish in action and tardy in obedience, than this which touches the possessions. Yet, on this point, the language of our Lord is as uncompromising, and His conditions as absolute and unavoidable, as on each that has gone before: "... whosoever he be of you that forsaketh not all that he hath, he cannot be my disciple." The reality, the complete fact, of true discipleship is still lacking and cannot exist, until this final condition is accepted and obeyed, until with the heart, the will and the life, the possessions also are given to Him.

As in the preceding stages of this inquiry, so in this portion also, we shall find it well to examine with careful minuteness the expressions uttered by the Master; both to avoid the error of a hasty judgment, that such a demand is practically out of reach, and to apprehend the real purpose He intended to affect in the disciple's life. Two words are employed in this sentence, which deserve exact study and particular definition, that the divine intention may be fully grasped: first that which is translated "forsaketh," and next, the one rendered "all that he hath." A clear grasp of the meaning attached to these words will serve to simplify the whole subject of the connection between the possessions of the Christian and his personal consecration to God.

Taking the latter of these two phrases, "all that he hath," we examine it with a view to discovering the real limits of the subject, with which consecration is here concerned. The three English words, "that he hath," are found with three other equivalents in the New Testament; all of which are of use and interest as serving to bring out the literal sense intended. In Luke 8:3, we read of certain women who accompanied Christ, and "ministered unto him of their substance…"; In Luke 11:21: "…his goods are in peace…"; Luke 16:1: "…had wasted his goods…"; Luke 19:8: "…the half of my goods…" A third equivalent is found in Luke 12:15, where the English is "…the things which he possesseth…" and in Acts 4:32: "…the things which he possessed…" Whilst the rendering of our text recurs in Luke 12:33; "Sell that ye have …"; 44, "…over all that he hath…"; Matthew 19:21, "…sell that thou hast…" A man's "substance," his "goods," "the things which he possesseth," and " all that he hath," form a comprehensive description of everything understood by the words "property, possessions, means, money, wealth, wages, income." The subject, therefore, includes everything which a person claims as or calls his own, outside the powers and faculties of the body and all that is within it.

This being the matter to be dealt with, the other word, forsaketh, explains what that dealing is to be. In Luke 9:61, a disciple asks that he may "…first go bid them farewell…"; and in Acts 18:21, it is said of Paul, that he "…bade them farewell…"; in which two passages to "bid farewell" represents the "forsaketh" of our text. Then in Acts 18:18, Paul "…took his leave…"; and in 2 Corinthians 2:13, describes himself as "… taking my leave of them …" Lastly, in Mark 6:46, where our Lord is dismissing the multitudes, we read, "… when He had sent them away …" in the sense of dismissing or bidding them farewell. The translation of the text, "forsaketh," does not occur elsewhere; as indeed the six passages named are the only places where the word occurs in the New Testament. These other three translations serve to throw a useful light upon the Master's condition of discipleship. They represent Him as bidding His followers to "bid farewell to," "take leave of," say good-bye to their possessions; as though renouncing their own rights of disposal over their property, and putting it into the charge of another.

A possible case in ordinary life may serve to illustrate this demand as a practical reality. The eldest son of a family has been lost at sea, and shortly after receipt of the news his father has died. The property is left by will to the eldest surviving son, and the second son of the family consequently takes possession, enjoys the inheritance, and makes full use of his wealth. After two years, the eldest son reappears, having been shipwrecked and cast ashore out of the ordinary track of vessels. What happens to the property? He is, of course, entitled to all that the second son has been possessing. But he bids his brother remain in possession as his own manager and representative, accounting to him for all the income and expending it according to his directions. From the day of the eldest son's reappearance, we should say that the second son "bade farewell" to the property; and the phrase would be equally true, even if he remained in charge of it as manager, and appeared outwardly in the same position as before. The eldest brother might alter his arrangements, but whatever these were, it would still be true, that the second brother had said good-bye to his ownership from the day of his brother's return.

Keeping this explanation in mind, we can now see clearly what this final condition of discipleship means. The Master has already claimed from everyone who would be His disciple, the first place in the affections, the submission of the will, the acceptance of His reproach, the surrender of the life to Him. Now His claim takes in one more thing, and declares that without it, discipleship is incomplete, nay, is non-existent. The disciple's possessions and property, all he called his own, are now to be put under another Owner; he is to bid farewell to his rights and authority over them; he is to forsake his position as proprietor; henceforth, they are the Master's, and he is only steward or treasurer over what he once called his own.

As in other conditions demanded from His disciples, so in this one also, the Master has fulfilled it Himself first, and has made Himself the pattern and example for His followers. At every stage of the Christian life we may read afresh: "I have given you an example, that ye should do as I have done to you" (John 13:15). If He demands the forsaking of all by us, it is no more than He did for us. "For ye know the grace of our Lord Jesus Christ, that, though he was rich, yet for your sakes he became poor, that ye through his poverty might be rich" (2 Cor. 8:9). It is probably also an illustration of His own conduct that is given in the parable of the "... treasure hid in a field; the which when a man hath found, he hideth, and for joy thereof goeth and selleth all that he hath, and buyeth that field" (Matt. 13:44). For the church is His "peculiar treasure," hid in the field of the world; for "the joy set before him" of gaining this church, He left all that He had and "emptied himself;" and by His redemption-work He "bought with a price" those whom He now calls "not their own." (Comp. Ps. 135:4 and Titus 2:14; Heb. 12:2; Phil. 2:7; 1 Cor. 6:20.)

This example of Christ Himself was followed also by His disciples and apostles, who could quietly and confidently appeal to Him, and find their appeal accepted and a blessing given to it, when they said: "'Behold, we have forsaken all, and followed thee ...'" (Matt. 19:27). It was, therefore, a condition, which those who first were called disciples fully accepted and faithfully fulfilled. It seemed to them a simple and natural thing, that at His command, all of earthly possessions should be let go, dealt with only by His command, in order wholly to follow Him. Paul is in the same position, when he writes of himself: "Yea doubtless, and I count all things *but* loss for the excellency of the knowledge of Christ Jesus my Lord; for whom I have suffered the loss of all things ..." (Phil. 3:8); and again describes himself "... as poor, yet making many rich; as having nothing, and *yet* possessing all things" (2 Cor. 6:10).

Personal Consecration

But not to the apostolic leaders and rulers of the early church was this obedience to the call, and acceptance of the conditions, of Christ confined; the whole church, in the first days of its Pentecostal fire, was equally ready and faithful to the Master's will. Immediately after Pentecost, the following description occurs of the conduct of the company of young disciples: "All that believed were together, and had all things common; And sold their possessions and goods, and parted them to all *men*, as every man had need" (Acts 2:44, 45). Presently, the further record follows: "And the multitude of them that believed were of one heart and of one soul: neither said any *of them* that ought of the things which he possessed was his own; but they had all things common … Neither was there any among them that lacked: for as many as were possessors of lands or houses sold them, and brought the prices of the things that were sold, And laid *them* down at the apostles' feet: and distribution was made unto every man according as he had need" (Acts 4:32, 34, 35). A condition of affairs prevailed thus in the early church, which afforded a picture of the most literal and exact obedience to the condition of discipleship under our view. If fulfillment of the Master's terms meant the right to be called His disciples, these were disciples indeed.

The apostolic precepts, given under the inspiration of the Holy Ghost, expanding and explaining the teaching and words of the Master, fully bear out the same view as to the "forsaking of all that he hath" by the disciple. They do not teach that the form in which this forsaking is to appear is always that of the church in Acts 2 and 4. There is no universal command given to all believers, that everyone must "sell all that he hath and give it to the poor," in order fully to follow Christ; though, even now, such a step may here and there be the personal call of God to an individual soul. But rather do we find the attitude impressed upon all true Christians, which is so concisely described above: "… neither said any *of them* that ought of the things which he possessed was his own …" (Acts 4:32). That conveys the very essence of this condition of discipleship, and presents, in a word, the practical issue of it in the life. "… what hast thou that thou didst not receive?" (1 Cor. 4:7) is the unanswerable question that explains the source, and origin and real ownership of all human possessions. The "rich in this world" are reminded that their riches are a gift and trust from God for the moment, to be used in good deeds, fair works, ready gifts and willing supply of the needs of others (1 Tim. 6:17, 18); and here, the last word, translated "willing to communicate," is of the same root as the word twice used above, where the disciples had all things "common" (Acts 2:44; 4:32). The same root reappears in the substantive form in Hebrews 13:16: "To do good and to communicate forget not: ... " the "communication" referred to being the use of so-called personal property for the common good of others. One who rightly so uses it has truly "forsaken" it for Christ's sake.

Peter presses home the same point, in reckoning all power for doing good to others as a gift entrusted by God, and for which the recipient is answerable as a "steward" or treasurer to the Giver. In the same way, Paul reckons the power to give, i.e., the possession of means, as one of the gifts imparted by God's grace, and to be used at God's command (1 Pet. 4:10; Rom. 12:8). The Word of God is consistent throughout in teaching, that earthly means and wealth are not a property, but a trust; over which a man is set not as owner, but as steward; and as much to be used by God's instructions and employed for God's service as the mightiest spiritual powers or intellectual talents.

But it is probably no exaggeration to say, that there is no topic upon which God's Word is more neglected, God's command more ignored, God's will more overlooked, God's principles more denied, amongst those who claim the title of Christian, than this of earthly possessions and temporal wealth. It is beyond dispute — it is a matter of plain figures and simple calculation — that this condition of discipleship is not accepted, this step in consecration is not taken, by the immense majority of those who "profess and call themselves Christians." It is only too apparent that our opening premise is true: The terms "Christian" and "disciple" are no longer coincident, synonymous, interchangeable. The claimants of the former title are the refusers of the latter. We may boldly assert, and do so with a sad abundance of evidence to confirm the truth of the assertion, that the condition of discipleship is no longer apparent in the church at large, by which a man "forsaketh all that he hath;" that the mark of the early disciples is no longer to be seen, when "neither said any *of them* that ought of the things which he possessed was his own." Rather does it appear that Christians are often indistinguishable from the world, in their bold assumption of undisputed ownership, and irresponsible rights, in what they call "the things they possess."

Are these things so? And if it cannot be denied, then ask again, Are these things right? Can it be right or well with a Christian, who practically ignores one of the Lord's conditions of discipleship? Let us put it to the test. If we ask in what way our possessions are practically to be "forsaken," and in reality "consecrated" to God, we must surely answer: By using them entirely under God's directions and according to His rules and principles. It becomes then a plain matter of obedience to the written Word. To this, as to every other duty in life, we should apply the question: "What is written in the law? How readest thou?" The Word of God gives abundant instruction: how to keep and use for Him whatever He entrusts us with; and to this Word, we must go for the practical directions in carrying out this demand to "forsake all that we have." That Word gives the general principles, by which we are put in the position of stewards or treasurers towards all our possessions; and also gives, for all who are willing to receive them, very particular and minute directions how those principles are to be applied.

Look first at that title of "steward" and see how it bears upon our subject. If one of us is made steward for some society, what a natural thing it is for us:

    a. to hold the funds entirely at the disposal of the society,
    b. to expend them only under the orders of the society, and
    c. to keep an accurate account of them for the use of the society.

How absurd it would be, and how indignantly we should refuse the proposal, if anyone suggested the use of those funds for our own private and personal ends. We should call it dishonesty, robbery, disgrace. Yet it seems to pass unchallenged by thousands of those who are God's stewards, when they use what He has put under their charge entirely at their own will and without any consideration of His will. This is the place where the wrong begins: the Christian cannot be Christ's disciple, unless he resigns the usurped place of owner and takes up the proper position of steward, towards the possessions with which God has entrusted him.

Then under the general heading of stewardship, the obedient disciple will find ample details of instruction concerning the use of his means in the pages of the New Testament, added to the permanent principles given in the Old. The barest outline must here suffice to show something of what God asks in the way of practical forsaking of our possessions; and it may serve to show to honest seekers, both the lines wherein they have failed in the past, and those upon which to commence at once a course of honest obedience. From the two great chapters on the use of means, in 2 Corinthians 8 and 9, we gather that the Master looks for an employment of His disciples' possessions, which is liberal (8:2), abundant (8:7), ready (8:11), willing (8:12), proportionate (8:12), systematic (9:5; cf. 1 Corinthians 16:2), bountiful (9:6), deliberate (9:7), cheerful (9:7). and such as to bring glory to God (9:13). Elsewhere, the special purposes for which these means are to be employed, over and beyond the supply of personal necessities of food and clothing (1 Tim. 6:8), are also defined with much exactness. They may be summed up under the heads of:

a. the provision for the family (2 Cor. 12:14);

b. the claims of relations (1 Tim. 5:8, 16);

c. the needs of the poor, and in especial of the poor saints in the church (Gal. 6:10);

d. the demands of hospitality (Rom. 12:13; Pet. 4:9);

e. the support of the ministry (Gal. 6:6; 1 Cor. 9:11; 1 Tim. 5:17, 18); and

f. the provision for missionaries (Phil. 4:16; 3 John 6, 7).

By practical obedience to such instructions, by our honest search into God's Word as to the how much, what on, and what for, of expenditure, there will be no need for doubt and uncertainty, and no lack of practical evidence, that our discipleship has stood the divine test and fulfilled the divine condition of "forsaking all that he hath," of consecrating the possessions to Christ.

In summary we note:

1. that the possessions are the last stage in consecration, in Old and New Testament alike;

2. that the claim includes everything outside himself which a man possesses;

3. that this is to be forsaken, bidden farewell to, for Christ;

4. that it means a transference of ownership from the disciple to the Master;

5. and the change in character from possessor to steward;

6. that Christ was herein our example;

7. that apostolic precept and practice illustrated it;

8. that the early church fulfilled it; and

9. that the New Testament contains the fullest instructions for the practical fulfillment of the demand.

Chapter 12
The Final Issue

"If ye know these things, happy are ye if ye do them."
(John 13:17)

THE various stages in the great fact of personal consecration have been passed in review, considered as equivalent to the conditions of discipleship laid down by our Lord for His first followers. There remains yet one question, by which the practical outcome of such teaching is brought to a point, and the real attitude of the whole church of Christ towards discipleship may fairly be ascertained and tested. We ask what the issue ought to be, where these conditions are honestly fulfilled; what our Lord meant to be the result of such discipleship; how it showed itself to be real. If we can succeed in defining the logical and necessary outcome of obedient discipleship, we can, at all times, discern whether the profession of Christianity is joined to the practice of discipleship and the reality of personal consecration.

Now there is one period of our Lord's life on earth, which, more than any other, serves to answer this question and supply the needful definition. Up to the time of His death, He was training His followers in the principles of discipleship, and leading them on gradually "as they were able to bear it"; with constant hints in the records of the training, that the disciples were slow in understanding, and dull in apprehending the lessons, and in putting them into practice. But after the Resurrection, there is a change in the character of the men, and of the instruction given by the Master. He seems to assume that the principles have now been at last apprehended, and their meaning illuminated by His own death and resurrection. He Himself opens their understandings that they might understand the Scriptures, and expounds in all the Scriptures the things concerning Himself. Thus are they prepared for the final issue of their whole calling, the practical outcome of consecration and discipleship, which forms in fact the one and only command received from their risen Lord. Five different reports are left us of the words of Christ after He rose from the dead, and the only command left to His church before His ascension: a command summed up in the phrase, the "Evangelization of the World."

Matthew gives the account of this command, as spoken by the Lord upon the mountain in Galilee, whither He had summoned the disciples to meet Him (Matt. 28:16–20). Mark's record places the command as apparently spoken first on the evening of the Resurrection-day (Mark 16:14–18); though perhaps his condensed narrative only conveys the gist of the great message, without meaning to define the time of its utterance. In Luke also, the first expression of the command seems connected with the day of the Resurrection, with an implied continuation of the topic on the way to the Ascension (Luke 24:44–50). John gives the commission in a short sentence, evidently uttered on that Easter evening (John 20:21). Luke, in the Acts, gives a full account of the form of the command on the day of Ascension (Acts 1:6–9). Thus, a fivefold emphasis is given to this command, which places it quite by itself for prominence and importance, and makes it fair to assume that the Lord meant it as a very summary and climax, a crowning point and final commission, to which all His previous teaching had been leading. A moment's thought over the consequent life of the disciples abundantly confirms this conviction. They evidently acted as if the very end and object of their discipleship was obedience to the command of their risen Lord. As evidently did they impress this meaning of discipleship upon their followers; and amid much of sad failure and decadence and error even in those early days, it is yet true in the main, that for the first three centuries after Christ, the whole church acted out the calling of Christ to His disciples, that they should carry the gospel to the whole world.

What then is the position of the church today towards this command of the Lord, and how does it stand in relation to this test of true discipleship? The whole witness of history has but one voice upon the subject, and that voice proclaims an almost universal neglect and total disregard of that command up to the eighteenth century. Then the first revival of recognition that this was the Lord's call appeared in the Moravian Church; and fifty years later, a similar faint revival began in England. That has spread and grown from small beginnings to a perceptible size; and coincidently, with the new movement of inquiry after God's principles of holiness and consecration, has come to assume larger proportions in the churches. Yet still, it is but a day of small things. The picture that the world presents today of the measure in which the church is obeying the Master's command, forms a sad contrast to the ardour of those early days. Let us seek an illustration. Suppose that a landowner gives an acre of land into a man's charge, with a full supply of all the necessaries, and orders him to bring that acre into cultivation and plant it according to instructions. The man begins, however, by fencing off half the acre and leaving it absolutely untouched. Then he divides the remainder into halves again, carelessly throws a few handfuls of seed upon the one portion, and sets himself thoroughly to work upon the last quarter acre. This he drains and cleans, ploughs and digs over, fertilizes and plants with much care. Fruit trees and shrubs, flowers and vegetables, roots and bulbs are thickly planted. The whole is tended and watered, enriched and watched over continually. Upon the already fully occupied ground, fresh seeds and new plants are continually being resown. Over the whole, he puts up a glass shelter; and then prides himself upon the exceeding attention he has given to the work. What will the master say when he comes? How long would he leave such a one in possession?

Yet this is an almost literally exact representation of the attitude of the church of Christ today. One half the population of the world is as yet unreached by the gospel. Of the remaining two-quarters, missionary work is but faintly touching the one which is not Christian; whilst upon the last quarter of professedly Christian lands, almost the whole energies of Christendom have been spent, and are being spent today. In England, there is an average of at least one clergyman or minister to every thousand of the population; whilst in the mission fields of the world, the average of missionaries (wives and female missionaries included) sent out by all the Christian churches of the world, do not yet reach a proportion of one to 100,000 of population. The contrast is awful, the neglect of the Lord's command appalling. What must He think now, what will He say by-and-by, when He comes to take account with His servants? It cannot be right that this should go on as it is. A remedy ought to be sought and applied by every true-hearted servant. And it will be found by each one, and by all, as they turn back to the first principles of consecration, and fulfill the old conditions of discipleship; by obedience to which the early church spread the gospel over the known world in the first centuries after Christ.

Placing side-by-side the needs of the world and the power of the gospel to meet them, it requires nothing but a consecrated church to bring the two together. Consecrated hearts will love what the Lord commands, and desire above all to fulfill it. Consecrated bodies and lives will go where He sends, and carry the message He gives throughout the wide world. Consecrated possessions will supply the needed funds and provide for the expense without difficulty. There are estimated to exist today no less than forty-million Christian communicants throughout the world: communicants, not merely nominal Christians who make no further profession than the name. Deduct what proportion you will from the forty million, as lifeless and loveless souls; allow that even half or three-quarters of them cannot be looked to for active sympathy with the Lord and His work; yet, surely, a quarter must be real in their knowledge of and love to the Lord. Now let that quarter, i.e., ten millions of Christians, rise up to respond to the Lord's call, consecrate themselves to His service, become His "disciples indeed"; and we know that there would be in them the power, the possibility and the possessions sufficient to evangelize the world before this generation has passed away.

It can be done. The Lord's Spirit is not straightened. What He did with "the early rain" at Pentecost sufficed to evangelize the known world then. If He does the same with "the latter rain" to prepare for His return now, the whole world can be evangelized within a generation. He spoke once to Israel as to the permanent presence of His Spirit among them, even when they had ceased to remember and profit by the blessing: "*According to* the word that I covenanted with you when ye came out of Egypt, so my spirit remaineth among you: fear ye not" (Hag. 2:5). The intervening thousand years had not impaired the power of the covenant nor broken the abiding reality of the Spirit's presence. So it is today. The promise and the gift of Pentecost are unbroken realities, perpetual truths, continuously present blessings, even though their existence has been forgotten, ignored, neglected. This is the power that can move the church, raise it up to consecration, recall it to discipleship today.

Again, the Lord spoke to Israel in immediate connection with the active working, indwelling and empowering of that Holy Spirit; and gave the one condition on which these would become realities: "Thus saith the Lord GOD: I will yet *for* this be enquired of by the house of Israel, to do *it* for them..." (Ezek. 36:37). His principles are the same, His character never alters: "I am the Lord. I change not." Therefore, the same power and working of the Holy Spirit are to be possessed and known today upon the same condition as of old. When the church as a whole asks for the promise of the Father, as it did in those early days, it will have the same answer, and result in the same devotion and glory to God. But the church is "the blessed company of all faithful people"; and what the church is bidden to do lies as a call upon each individual heart.

So is it with the subject of this book. It is a call to all, but it is only obeyed when recognized as a call to each one singly. There was a time when the Moravian Church was 120,000 marks in debt; and special contributions were asked from all members. A humble shoemaker was called upon for help, and he gave this answer: "There are 30,000 members of our church, and 120,000 marks of debt: that is four marks apiece. Here we are, myself, my wife, and five children; that is 7. Seven times 4 are 28; and here is my share, 28 marks." Next year the debt had been diminished, but was not gone. The collector came again and reported still a debt of 90,000 marks. The simple cobbler never stayed to grumble at the slackness of other members, but answered again: "That is an average of 3 marks for each member. Thank God, wife and children are still here: so 7 times 3 are 21; and here is my share of 21 marks." That is the true spirit in which to hear God's call, and do His will. May He grant us to quiet all doubts or delays or questionings about others, and faithfully to do our own share, saying as He did of old, when questioned by one about the future of another disciple: "...what *is that* to thee? follow thou me" (John 21:22).

Personal Consecration

In conclusion, let us remember:

1. that there is a test by which the reality of discipleship is proved;

2. that it forms the substance of the teaching of the Lord after He rose from the dead;

3. that it is contained in the one command, to evangelize the world;

4. that this command was obeyed at the beginning, and utterly neglected in the middle of this dispensation;

5. that a return to the obedience of early disciples, and reality of their consecration, will mean renewed enthusiasm for missionary work; and

6. that the power and the presence of the Holy Ghost are assured, will be given, and can effectually complete the work, through praying, obedient, and consecrated souls.